HOW TO PLAN & BUILD
BOOKCASES, CABINETS
& SHELVES

*Created and designed by
the editorial staff of
ORTHO BOOKS*

Project Editor
Karin Shakery

Writer
Craig Bergquist

Illustrator
Gene Takeshita

Photographer
Kit Morris

Photographic Stylist
Sara Slavin

Ortho Books

Publisher
Robert J. Dolezal

Production Director
Ernie S. Tasaki

Managing Editors
Karin Shakery
Michael D. Smith
Sally W. Smith

System Manager
Leonard D. Grotta

National Sales Manager
Charles H. Aydelotte

Marketing Specialist
Susan B. Boyle

Operations Coordinator
Georgiann Wright

Administrative Assistant
Deborah Tibbetts

Senior Technical Analyst
J. A. Crozier, Jr.

Address all inquiries to
Ortho Books
Chevron Chemical Company
Consumer Products Division
575 Market Street
San Francisco, CA 94105

Copyright © 1987
Chevron Chemical Company
All rights reserved under international and Pan-American copyright conventions.

1 2 3 4 5 6 7 8 9
87 88 89 90 91 92

ISBN 0-89721-088-3
Library of Congress Catalog Card
Number 86-072432

Chevron

Chevron Chemical Company
575 Market Street, San Francisco, CA 94105

Acknowledgments

Copy Chief
Melinda Levine

Copyeditor
Judith Dunham

Editorial Assistant
Andrea Y. Connolly

Proofreader
Leslie Tilley

Production Coordinator
Linda M. Bouchard

Production Artist
Lezlly Freier

Indexer
Elinor Lindheimer

Lithographed in USA by
Webcrafters, Inc.

Designers & Architects

John Marsh Davis
Sausalito, Calif.
Pages 4–5

Ralph Frischman
San Francisco, Calif.
Pages 9, 11, 70–71

Arnelle Kase/Barbara Scavullo Design
San Francisco, Calif.
Pages 3, 7, 8, 18

Judith Kimball
San Francisco, Calif.
Pages 3, 49

Jamie Millican
Berkeley, Calif.
Page 23

Osburn Design
San Francisco, Calif.
Pages 12–13

Tony Pisacane
San Francisco, Calif.
Pages 3, 10, 21, 29, 51

Karen Sheehan
San Francisco, Calif.
Page 49

Robert Steffy
San Francisco, Calif.
Pages 34–35

Additional Photographers

California Redwood Assoc./
 Peter Christiansen, 12–13
Doug Manchee, 15
Donna Kempner, 23
Stephen Marley, 30, 44

Special Thanks

Howard Blechman
California Redwood Assoc.
Dona Candela
Nancy and Harvey Epstein
Brian Firestone
Arnelle Kase
Judith and Charles Kimball
Robert Steffy
Myralin Whitaker

Front cover. Cubes can be used to separate and organize collections. Build a case following directions that start on page 88 or buy unfinished cubes and stabilize them as described on page 75.

Back cover
Above left. Bookcases and shelves can enliven the architecture of a room as well as provide storage.
Above right. A simple cabinet takes on a special look when ornamented with bun feet and a raised top.
Below left. Glass shelves in an illuminated case display a collection of antique toys.
Below right. To allow for more efficient shelf space, this corner cabinet is not actually triangular (see page 91).

Page 1. Small shelves attached to the side wall of a cabinet provide display space for treasured objects.

Page 3
Above. Shallow shelves above a refrigerator are ideal for storing large, flat items such as baking sheets and trays.
Below. To prevent shelves from sagging under the weight of a load of heavy books, make sure the span is not too great and the shelf material is strong enough and well supported.

HOW TO PLAN & BUILD
BOOKCASES, CABINETS & SHELVES

MAKING PLANS

B ookcases, cabinets, and shelves will store a variety of items, fill empty corners, make a dramatic focal point in a room, and provide a place to display a collection. Record albums, books, kitchen equipment and supplies, toys, linens, and paraphernalia for drinks are just some of the items that can be either displayed or concealed.

Design considerations and basic structure of a bookcase are very similar to those of a cabinet. Therefore, the term "case" refers to both pieces.

Building a case is an excellent introduction to the satisfactions of working with wood. It is a relatively easy project and one that will yield practical and handsome results.

Staggered heights of these bookcases add importance to the doorway and emphasize the lines of the pitched roof. Deeper shelves create a desk on one side, an entertainment center on the other.

GETTING STARTED

This book provides the means to make a variety of bookcases and cabinets. What you need to know in order to plan and to execute a project is explained and many options are presented. Then it is up to you how closely you follow the plans; you can adapt them, add any of the options suggested, or mix and match ideas, developing your own design.

All you need in order to create a case that uniquely suits your needs and tastes is to master some basic construction techniques.

Realize that with care, patience, and a respect for materials and tools, a lack of refined carpentry skills can be overcome. However, beginners should not start out by taking on a complicated project. There is more pleasure in building a simple box well than there is in doing an inferior job on an intricate piece.

If you lack the confidence to plunge directly into a project, find some good-sized pieces of scrap wood. Use them to learn how to handle tools and to see how the material responds. This way you'll know what to expect when you work on a project that counts.

Defining your needs
When thinking about your needs, consider three basic functions that cases can fulfill:

Access. A properly designed case stores its contents in an organized way so that they can be quickly found and retrieved and the order of the other stored items is not disrupted. Cases can be designed to house kitchenware, tools, camera equipment, and toys.

Display. Fragile items and objects that should be protected from dust—china collections and model ships, for example—are best presented in glass-fronted cabinets. Stereo equipment can be displayed to best advantage in a special cabinet, although glass doors are more of an option than a necessity.

Protection. Dangerous chemicals such as pesticides, herbicides, and strong cleaning agents must be kept safely away from youngsters. A locked cabinet in the garage might be a practical solution, but several such cabinets—located in the kitchen, laundry room, garage, and shed—might be even better. Liquor and guns in the home should also be securely kept from children. Special cabinets can be designed for these purposes or existing cabinets can be modified using the suggestions.

Considering your options
In order to create a case you'll be pleased with, take the time to make a detailed plan. The following questions need to be considered.
☐ Where will it go?
☐ How big should it be?
☐ What should it be made of?
☐ Should the shelves be fixed or adjustable?
☐ How should it be finished?

After carefully assessing your needs, wants, and priorities, you'll find that the choices will practically make themselves.

Four main considerations will affect all of your decisions:

Money
Know what you are willing to spend. Cost may dictate certain design decisions, rule out particular materials, or limit the size of the project. Building your own case will not necessarily save you money, especially if you apply a monetary value to time.

If you lack access to a well-equipped shop, you have to include the cost of any tools you must buy, as well as the money spent on materials. However, building your own case offers rewards that can't be had by picking out a ready-made piece at the store and driving it home. You won't get the enjoyment of working with your hands and the satisfaction of doing a job well. Further, it is doubtful that you will find a ready-made piece that is exactly the right size and finish.

Time
Building a case takes time. The more elaborate the design, the more time it will take. Rushing not only increases the likelihood of mistakes and frustration but makes the construction process more a chore than a pleasure. Always be realistic about the amount of time you're willing to spend.

Skills
If you are a novice, start with simple designs and techniques. Try more complicated projects as you grow more comfortable with tools and learn more about the characteristics of the various materials.

Work space
Some projects are simple to make even if you live in an apartment—a spare corner or utility room can be a shop. For projects in such limited spaces, all the pieces should be precut at the lumberyard so that only assembly and finishing are needed. Do not attempt a large project or one that will take a long time to complete. Instead, try a small cabinet (page 78) or a simple bookcase (page 80).

If a shop or work area in your garage or basement is available, it's not necessary to limit your projects; just make sure that large projects will fit through the doors and around the corners encountered between the shop and destination.

SELECTING A STYLE

Having decided on the amount of money, time, skill, and space available, you can now concentrate on selecting the right design.

Location, more than intended use, should determine the style you choose. If making a built-in case, you will almost certainly want to match the existing look of the area. Find trim that matches the molding and, if possible, knobs that either match or complement the others in the room.

Building a freestanding case opens many design possibilities. You can make a case that blends in with the existing furniture or use the new case to make a design statement—perhaps to set a new tone for the decor of the room. The photographs in this chapter show a wide variety of styles and are meant to serve as an idea book. If you see a style you like, plan to apply that style to the case you design, but first make some sketches to help you envision the completed project.

Choosing a location

The room in which the bookcase or cabinet is to be used will determine some of your decisions.

Living room. Living-room shelves and cabinets should be well designed, constructed from attractive materials, and finely crafted with adjustable shelves for displaying books and art objects of various sizes. Cases for stereo or video equipment look clean and uncluttered when holes are made for routing wires.

Dining room. Cabinets will probably be used to store china and linens. Make sure shelves and drawers are deep enough and wide enough to house these items.

The dining room might also be the place for a bar cabinet. This could be an open case lined with mirrors and fitted with shelves, or a closed cabinet with doors painted to match the

In keeping with the playful attitudes of the current architectural styles, these built-in shelves and cabinets make a more interesting statement than would an ordinary rectanglar shape.

walls or made of wood that matches the dining table.

Den and library. These rooms may need several cases and cabinets to house books, a record collection, board games, and sewing supplies. Cases should be designed to incorporate areas that will show off attractive objects while concealing utilitarian ones.

Playroom. For a child's playroom, you will probably want a simple, functional piece of furniture made of durable materials and finished with a painted, easy-to-clean surface.

Kitchen. Kitchen shelves should be fully adjustable for the most efficient use of space. The deeper shelves will accommodate cookware and small appliances, and vertically divided spaces are useful for storing trays and cookie sheets.

The finish should be easy to keep clean. Use paint that matches the walls, a clear polyurethane finish, or face the doors with plastic laminate.

Bathroom. As in the kitchen, bathroom surfaces must be easy to keep clean. In addition the materials must be able to withstand moisture.

Most people find that several small drawers are more practical for storing toiletries than a few large ones. Small drawers also make it easier to fit storage areas around plumbing pipes and fixtures.

Workshop. In a workshop you'll probably want fixed shelves in rugged materials that will take wear and tear and dirt. This is not the place for expensive, exotic woods.

Utility room. Like a workshop, this is a place where practicality is the main consideration. Shelves should be large enough to hold economy-sized cleaning supplies.

If this room also houses laundry equipment, make sure that space is provided for baskets, iron, and ironing board.

Entry. When decorating a home, don't overlook the potential of an entrance hall. Considering that it is responsible for the first impression guests have of your house, it is a good place to make a statement.

This can be done by using a case filled with a special collection.

Corridor. If you have a corridor that is fairly wide, a row of bookcases can be a handsome and practical addition to a long corridor. It will visually foreshorten the corridor as well as add decorative interest.

Garage and shed. In addition to sturdy shelves for bulky items such as yard, patio, and outdoor equipment, these locations should have cabinets with locks if you will be storing insecticides, cleaning agents, and other dangerous chemicals.

Above: *Standard bathroom cabinets rarely allow for enough storage. When you make your own, not only can you put in as many drawers and shelves as will fit, but you can size them to suit particular needs.*
Opposite: *These built-ins required careful planning, measuring, and constructing as well as a saber saw to cut the curved edges.*

T*he dimensions of a case depend on the space available. Look closely at the room. Is there unused wall space? Is there a place for a freestanding unit?*

Matching what exists

The best design echoes already existing lines. For example, a bookcase consistent with the height of windows or doors looks as if it belongs in the room. Positioning shelves along the same plane as the height of a table or at the same level as a sofa arm relates them to the furnishings. Building cabinets around a radiator disguises or at least deemphasizes it. But don't enclose a radiator, or you will end up with a hot cabinet and a cold room!

Practicality

Don't build shelves that you are unable to reach or ones that force you to stoop awkwardly when you retrieve objects or put them away. Remember that even though you might be able to reach a high shelf, you will only be able to see the larger items on the shelf. Small items will be out of sight. Consider putting drawers or slide-out shelves inside low cabinets to increase convenience.

Cases should be accessible and should allow access to heat vents, light switches, electrical outlets, and pieces of furniture.

Think ahead, plan on paper, and experiment by positioning large cardboard boxes in the location proposed for a case. Do not place a bookcase or cabinet in a spot where it will be bumped every time someone enters the room.

Assessing the storage

What are you planning to put on the shelves or inside the compartments? Art books? Paperbacks? Children's toys? Stereo equipment? A television? Answering these questions will enable you to determine how deep the shelves must be, how far apart they should be, and how strong they need to be.

Pages 36–69 show how to construct special features, such as a wine rack, slide-out TV shelf, sewing center, and computer area. You can build these features into almost any bookcase or cabinet, thereby customizing the structure to suit all of your particular needs.

If the case is intended for storage, measure the items you want to accommodate. It may not bother you that your record albums (12½ inches square) will stick out beyond the edge of an 11½-inch shelf, but you should know this before building.

Opposite: Always consider the placement before starting to build. Here the cabinets and the shelves that float above them are sized to fit between door and fireplace.

Above: To avoid ugly sagging, heavy magazines, books, or records should never be arranged on shelves that are more than 30 inches wide unless the shelves are strengthened or supported.

PLOTTING MOVES

H aving planned what you are going to build and where you are going to put it, the next step is to familiarize yourself with general construction methods for finish carpentry.

First make sure you have finalized your design. Not only will this affect the type and amount of material you need to order, it may change the sequence in which you do the work.

With plans in hand, you are ready to decide how to proceed. Check that you have all the necessary tools; familiarize yourself with techniques; and choose an applicable finish.

Making furniture is a particularly rewarding project if the job goes smoothly and the results warrant the effort.

An unusual system is created by lining the walls with redwood boards, allowing deep grooves at regular intervals. Cleats, attached to the backs of the redwood boxes, drop into these grooves.

MATERIALS

Bookcases, cabinets, shelves, and doors can be constructed from a variety of materials, including metal, plastic, and glass, but wood and wood products are by far the most versatile and most commonly used.

Wood

There are four basic choices of wood: softwood, hardwood, plywood, and particleboard (also called chipboard). Each has advantages and disadvantages (see chart on page 16). Your choice should be based on the requirements of your project, your budget, and your skills.

Visit a local lumberyard, see the stock carried, poke around, and don't be afraid to ask questions. The more you look at the different types of wood, touch them, and learn about them, the more comfortable you will feel when making a selection.

The availability of particular woods varies greatly from area to area, so a trip to a nearby lumberyard is the best way to assess your choices.

Softwood

This is lumber from coniferous trees and includes pine, fir, redwood, hemlock, cedar, and spruce. It is generally easier to work with and less expensive than hardwood.

Hardwood

Hardwood comes from deciduous trees, the broad-leafed types that lose their leaves in the winter: oak, birch, cherry, maple, and walnut. Despite the name, the wood is not always hard. Basswood, or linden, is a hardwood, and so is balsa wood, which is extremely soft.

Hardwoods are generally harder in at least two respects: They are harder to work with and harder to find. They also tend to be expensive. Carpenters, however, prize them for their handsome colors and grains, their strength, and their durability. Hardwoods can be finely and precisely worked and take finishes very well.

Plywood

Plywood is a manufactured product. A special saw shaves the wood from the log in a continuous sheet, which looks somewhat like a roll of paper towels unfurling from its cardboard core. The thin sheets, or plies, are glued together face-to-face, under pressure, with the grain running in alternate directions. This gives plywood considerable strength and resistance to warping. These features, along with relatively low cost, make plywood a widely used material.

You can buy both softwood and hardwood plywoods. Softwood plywoods, most often made of Douglas fir, are usually softwood throughout. Hardwood plywoods are likely to have softwood or particleboard cores and only the outermost plies made of hardwood.

Thin sheets of plywood, usually ⅛ inch to ¼ inch thick, are commonly used as back panels on cases. The thinnest plywood available is known as door skin. It is available in ⅛-inch 3 by 7 sheets with a birch veneer on one side and mahogany on the other. Sounds expensive, but a door skin costs only about five dollars.

Particleboard

This material, also called chipboard, is created by combining wood fibers and particles with glue and pressing the mixture into panels. The result is a hard, heavy, inexpensive material. It does not look like wood and is most suitable for projects where cost and durability are more important than appearance.

Particleboard can be difficult to work with because it resists nails and screws and dulls blades. Choose the denser industrial grade rather than the type intended for subflooring.

Amount needed

Once you've decided on the type of wood you want to use, you must figure out how much to buy. There are detailed materials lists for the projects in this book, but if you're changing the given dimensions or designing your own project, you'll have to estimate the quantities needed for the design.

First sketch out the design. Draw the front view, side view, perhaps top and back views, and indicate the dimensions. Do this on graph paper so that it can be drawn to scale. Make a list showing each piece of wood needed, its place in the construction (side wall, shelf, etc.), and its measurements. Then summarize the list so that you know how many pieces of each size you'll need to purchase. (Carpenters sometimes call this list a stock bill.)

As you compute the dimensions of the project, don't forget to allow for the dimensions of the lumber. Suppose, for instance, that the bookcase is 36 inches wide, with sides made out of 2 by 12 boards and shelves that butt or are supported on cleats. In this example, the shelves are only 33 inches long—a difference of 3 rather than 4 inches because a 2 by 12 is actually only 1½ inches thick. Adjustable shelves should be ⅛ inch shorter so that they are easier to set in place. On the other hand, dadoed shelves (shelves mounted in grooves cut across the side panels) need to be longer. The length depends on the depth of the grooves.

When you know what you need, figure out the most efficient way to buy the correct amount of wood. If you're using lumber, this is fairly easy. You'll want so many boards of this length and so many of that length. Realize, though, that it might work out more economically to buy a longer or wider board and cut smaller pieces from it.

Plywood and particleboard are usually sold in 4 by 8 sheets. Sketch out those dimensions to scale on graph paper. Figure out how you can lay out the pieces to make the best use of the sheet. Remember to allow a small amount for the kerf (the wood that is lost due to the saw cut).

Making a layout is like putting together a jigsaw puzzle; the aim is to make as few cuts as possible and keep waste to a minimum. Try to plan your layout so that leftovers are in one big piece rather than many small scraps. This way there will be material on hand for the next project.

If you are intending to use a clear finish on the project, consider the direction of the grain as you plan the layout. Shelves look much better if they are cut so that the grain always runs in the same direction.

Allow a little extra wood for mistakes. Even professionals make them, and it is a nuisance to have to return to the lumberyard for more material.

Wood grades

Methods for grading wood products are complex. Grading symbols vary according to the type of wood graded, whether it is hardwood, softwood, or plywood, and the symbols aren't always standardized, even within a category.

When picking boards or sheets for a case, trust your eye. If you look carefully, you will be able to pick the right grade. If you don't trust your own judgment, ask for help. Tell the salesperson exactly what you are planning to make.

Grades of wood are a measure of

the allowable defects. Boards should have as few defects as possible, although there is some latitude. For instance, knots may be acceptable if you plan to paint your case and are willing to do the filling and sanding needed to overcome any oiliness and rough texture. It is possible that you might like the look of knotty wood. You might also be less concerned about flaws that will be hidden from view when your case is full.

Wood that is used in general construction, such as 2 by 4s and other dimensional lumber, is often sold green. It will shrink as it dries.

For your projects, however, you will want to purchase wood that has already been dried. This is called kiln-dried, KD, or seasoned wood, and it is always stored indoors at the lumberyard, although not always in a heated area.

If you aren't sure whether the wood you are selecting will be suitable for cabinetry, ask the salesperson before buying it.

Doors can be finished in any number of ways ranging from staining to laminating to painting. This unusual treatment combines rough-sawn plywood with high-gloss enamel. The result is a sleek but highly textured look. Because the plywood is finished with polyurethane, doors can be brushed clean.

Materials chart

	Softwood	Hardwood	Plywood	Particleboard
Cost	Inexpensive (to moderately expensive for clear kiln-dried wood)	Expensive	Inexpensive (to moderately expensive for solid-core and hardwood-veneered plywood)	Inexpensive
Availability	Widely available as moldings as well as straight stock up to 2x12	Available at hardwood outlets, and some lumberyards, as moldings and stock in varying sizes up to 4x12	Widely available in 4x8 sheets (⅛″ to 1¼″ thick) sanded softwood or hardwood outer veneers	Widely available in 4x8 sheets (⅛″ to 1″ thick). Some surface texture. Available in 3 densities
Quality	Buyer should choose stock carefully	Buyer should choose stock carefully	Quality indicated by grade stamp (A = high, D = low)	Very consistent quality
Strength	Medium strength	Generally very strong	Will flex but resists breaking	Will flex and break
Characteristics	Easy to work, requires care to avoid marring wood in shop	Easy to work, but requires very sharp tools and more time than softwood	Requires special blade for proper cutting, edges remain rough and must be covered or treated for finished appearance unless solid core is used	Requires special blade for proper cutting, edges can be shaped with router, but remain slightly textured
Gluing	Good	Mostly good, except for oily woods like teak and eucalyptus	Good	Good
Sanding	Easy to sand	Careful sanding yields superior results	Sanded during manufacture, but can be improved using sanding sealer and fine paper	Sanding yields only slight reduction in surface texture
Painting	Excellent, use sealer primer first	Good, but porous woods require a filler before painting	Good, use sealer primer first	Good, but some texture will be evident
Clear Finishing	Good	Good	Softwood grain not always attractive. Hardwood plywood gives good finish	Utility only

Wood defects

When selecting lengths of wood, check them carefully to be sure there are none of the following defects.

Knots. These dense spots, usually darker than the surrounding wood, form where a branch grows from the trunk of the tree. A tight knot might only affect appearance, but loose knots and knotholes weaken the board structurally. Avoid too many knots. Wood that is free of knots is called clear.

Checks. These are small cracks in the board that run across the annual growth rings of the tree.

Splits. Splits, a more serious version of checks, extend all the way through the board.

Shakes. This term refers to separations, where layers of wood are beginning to peel apart between the growth rings.

Wanes. Sometimes the edges of a board aren't square and look angled or beveled. This generally means that the board was cut from the outside part of the tree; occasionally bark still runs along the wane.

Cups, twists, crooks, and bows. These are the result of different types of warping, usually caused by improper drying. Always avoid boards with these defects.

Pitch pockets. A pitch pocket is a resin-filled cavity found in some softwoods. Often the resin, or pitch, continues to ooze. Boards laden with pitch are heavy and tend to split.

Color and grain

The color of wood varies according to the species of the tree from which it comes. Hardwoods and softwoods are found in a full range of colors, and no one wood is inherently better than another. Choose whatever pleases you, keeping in mind the finish that you plan to use on the wood. Some woods display dramatic grain patterns after a finish is applied   pat

terns that are almost unnoticeable on the raw wood.

Grain is the pattern made by the annual growth rings of the tree. It varies depending on the species and on how the particular board was cut.

Flat-grain boards are milled so that the grain runs parallel to the face of the board. These boards are more common because many can be cut from the log. On vertical-grain boards, the grain runs perpendicular to the face.

Although flat-grain cuts sometimes yield a dramatic, swirly pattern, the boards are more prone to shrink and are not as strong as vertical-grain boards. Therefore, flat-grain boards are considered to be of lower quality.

Dimensions of lumber

Lumber is sold according to a set of dimensions known as nominal size. Nominal refers to the name that the lumber bears. For example, although a board was originally cut to 2 inches thick by 4 inches wide (and named a 2 by 4), it will be less than that size when purchased. Due to shrinkage and variations in milling, a 2 by 4 usually measures 1½ by 3½ inches. The true dimensions are called actual size; when drawing up plans, you should be aware of the difference.

Other measuring terms you'll come across at the lumberyard are board feet and linear feet. The linear-foot measurement is simply the length of the board.

Board feet are computed with a formula that gives the total volume of the wood. One board foot is the amount of wood that is in a piece one foot long, one foot wide, and one inch thick.

Example. A 10-foot-long 2 by 8 would be 13.34 board feet:
10 x 2 x .667 = 13.34.

Board feet are only used by contractors and carpenters when ordering lumber in large quantities.

Nonstructural materials

Some materials are selected for economy (veneers), protection (plastic laminates), or decoration (moldings).

Veneers

A thin skin shaved or sliced from a log of premium wood, the veneer is glued over a particleboard, plywood, or softwood structure to give the appearance that the entire case is actually made of the veneer material. It's also possible to use several different veneers to create a pattern on a case.

Plastic laminates

For surfaces that must stand up to wear and tear and constant cleaning, sheet laminates may be the answer.

Laminates are available in a variety of colors. The two grades most useful to the do-it-yourselfer are the general-purpose grade (¹/₁₆ inch thick), and the vertical grade (half as thick and not quite as durable). If you intend to use plastic laminate on thin, unsupported panels such as cabinet doors, adhere laminate to both sides of the panel to keep it from warping due to uneven moisture absorption.

Moldings

A wide range of decorative moldings milled from softwood, usually pine, are available. Hardwood molding is also available, but it may be difficult to find much variety.

Carvings and wood castings

You may find a use for a carving, such as a newel cap atop a fancy bookcase, but more likely, if you are building an elaborate piece, you will choose a wood casting. These castings can be glued to cabinet surfaces for a dramatic accent or as a decorative band of beading.

Turnings

Spindles and caps are decorative elements only used on cabinets occasionally. When they are used, they are often sliced in half lengthwise and glued to the front surface.

HAND TOOLS

Tools fall into three categories: hand tools, such as hammers, screwdrivers, chisels, and squares; hand-held power tools, such as electric drills and saber saws; and stationary power tools that are larger, hard-to-move machines, such as table saws and radial arm saws.

Good tools are a good investment. You can build your collection gradually as you build your skills, but always buy quality. Inferior tools make it extremely difficult to do good work, and they continually have to be replaced. Once you have good tools, take care of them. Keep them oiled, clean, and sharp.

Lumberyards, home centers, and hardware stores are the places where you will be selecting most of your tools, but don't overlook two other sources: mail order and flea markets. Popular do-it-yourself magazines carry ads for mail-order tools and hardware. Order catalogs first, and when selecting tools, stick with name brands to be safe. Many estate-sale tools end up at the flea market. Hand tools will predominate, and many of these older, well-made tools will stand up to several generations of use.

Despite the value of power tools, a good set of hand tools is the backbone of any woodworking shop, and you can't claim to be a good carpenter if you're unable to use them.

The projects in this book call for the tools listed below, and these are all that are actually necessary. However, working with only these would make the building process much

Having the right tools and using them properly can turn a do-it-yourselfer into a carpenter. Before trying to duplicate the skillful shapes incorporated into this bathroom vanity, make sure that you have mastered the tools and techniques required.

slower and more laborious. If you are building a bookcase with hand tools, think seriously about having boards cut to size at the lumberyard.

Measuring tool
Accurate measurements are essential to the success of any construction project. Both a retractable metal tape measure and a carpenter's folding rule will come in handy.

Hammer
A 16-ounce curved-claw hammer is probably the most useful all-around hammer for a home workshop. Lift and swing the ones at the hardware store to see what feels comfortable for you. A 5-ounce magnetized tack hammer is useful for driving brads and working in tight places. For setting tight joints and general wood persuasion, a rubber mallet is a must.

Screwdriver

You should own several flat-blade screwdrivers to handle different-sized slotted screws. Special straight-sided screwdrivers are used to tighten screws inside a counterbore. Phillips screws require Phillips screwdrivers.

Awl

The pointed tip of this useful tool will mark stock and make holes for starting small screws.

Try square/combination square

Use these for making sure that corners are square, marking cut lines on boards, and taking measurements. Combination squares have built-in spirit levels and can be used as a marking gauge as well.

Carpenter's level

This will help determine whether the work is level (on horizontal surfaces) and plumb (on vertical surfaces).

Handsaw

The familiar-looking handsaw comes in two versions: the crosscut saw for cutting across the grain of the wood and the ripsaw for cutting along the grain. The two look very similar; the difference is the configuration of the teeth. Often the blade is stamped with the type that it is. A crosscut saw is the most useful.

Backsaw

Although the handle shapes vary, all backsaws have a rectangular blade and a reinforced backbone along the top. The smaller versions—tenon saws and dovetail saws—are used for hand-cutting those joints respectively. The larger backsaw is the type of saw used with a miter box.

Miter box

This slotted box holds the saw blade at a particular angle (commonly 90 degrees and 45 degrees), so that a precise cut can be made.

Plane

A plane shaves wood to smooth, square, and flatten it. The general-use jack plane works in the direction of the grain of the wood. The smaller block plane is used for shaping the ends of boards, rounded surfaces, and spots too small for the jack plane to handle.

Chisel

The beveled blade of this tool makes it possible to remove excess wood from notches and grooves. It can also be used to trim off the protruding tops of wood plugs that cover countersunk screws. Chisels are available in various widths. They can be purchased individually or as a set, but in any case, make sure to have ¼-inch, ½-inch, and ¾-inch chisels.

File and rasp

For cleaning up cut surfaces and creating irregular shapes, it's a good idea to have a selection of files and rasps on hand. The single-cut files are used for tool maintenance as well as for wood removal, but rasps, with individual triangular teeth, are meant for wood only. Use the rasp for rough work. The file, especially the single cut, will produce a smoother surface. Rifflers are small curved rasps used to clean out and finish carvings.

The Surform® is a modern, rasplike tool. It comes in several models with replaceable blades of either stamped steel or abrasive grit.

Sanding block

Wrapping abrasive paper around a sanding block makes hand-sanding easier. Blocks that hold the abrasive paper securely and are shaped for a comfortable grip can be purchased. However, any block of wood that fits the hand will do the job.

Scraping plate

A simple 3-inch by 5-inch steel plate, scraping plate, or cabinet scraper takes the place of abrasive paper on some jobs—and with better results. It's necessary, however, to learn the sharpening technique to renew the scraper edges when they dull.

Clamp

Clamps will hold a glued joint securely while the adhesive sets. There are a variety of types including bar, spring, miter, and C-clamps. Each has a specific function. The C-clamp, which resembles the letter it is named for, is the most common type found in a carpentry shop.

Vise

Mounted on the workbench, the vise will hold a board firmly while it is worked on. The woodworking vise, with larger, wood faces, is preferred to the basic shop vise, but either kind will do.

Hand drill or bit brace

If you don't plan to get an electric drill, use either of these tools to drill holes. Operating a hand drill is a bit like using an eggbeater. The bit brace is turned by a ratchet and a sweeping, U-shaped handle.

Doweling jig

This device clamps onto a board and acts as a guide for drilling straight, perpendicular holes. It works best if both boards to be doweled are clamped together and then drilled in succession without relocating the clamp. If one set of holes must be drilled first, place dowel centers in them to mark the second board for drilling.

Whetstone

A whetstone is useful for keeping a sharp edge on bladed tools—particularly chisels. When sharpening on a whetstone, be sure you maintain the bevel at the proper angle.

POWER TOOLS

*S*ome artisans would have you believe that using power tools is cheating. It's true that any woodworking project can be constructed with hand tools; carpenters worked this way for centuries before electrical equipment was invented. The houses they built kept out the rain, and the tables and chairs they made were sturdy and often very beautiful.

Using only hand tools, however, requires a high level of skill, a strong dedication to craftsmanship, and a lot of time. Most woodworkers find that investing in at least a few power tools pays off in accuracy and efficiency without reducing the pride and pleasure in their work.

If you don't own a complete tool collection, you can rent what you need or the lumberyard can cut wood to size for you. Maybe you know someone you can borrow tools from—and possibly receive instruction on their use as well.

Portable power tools
To make the projects in this book, the basic hand tools described on the previous pages will be needed. If you also own the following portable power tools the work will go more smoothly and more quickly.

Electric drill
If you're going to purchase only one power tool, it probably should be a drill. This versatile piece of equipment has many accessories that allow a great deal more than just drilling.

With the right attachments, you can sand, plane, cut large holes and straight lines, drive and countersink screws, cut plugs to fill screw holes, and even mix paint.

Electric drills are sized according to the shank of the largest bit they are able to accommodate. A ⅜-inch, variable-speed model would be a good choice. Comparative quality is often reflected in the amp ratings of the motors. Higher amperage means more power and greater flexibility.

In addition to a basic set of twist drills the combination bit for screws will prove useful for the projects in this book. Normally, when driving a screw, first make a pilot hole slightly smaller than the screw shank. (This allows the screw to penetrate the wood and bite in firmly.) Then make a countersink hole large enough to accommodate the screw head and deep enough so that the head sets just below the surface. The combination bit will drill both at once. Be sure the bit matches the size of the screws. Hold the bit on top of the screw. The shank of the screw should be completely hidden by the drill bit; only the threads should show.

Router
With a router, you can cut grooves and channels, and shape edges of boards, and trim veneers and laminates. It is used in cabinetry for making fine joints such as dadoes and rabbets (see page 25) and shaping moldings.

Because a router can be tricky to use at first, try practicing on scrap lumber. Once familiar it will be invaluable for doing fancy cutting with a minimum of fuss.

Power handsaw
If you are purchasing a general-purpose saw for construction as well as cabinetry, then the circular saw is the saw of choice. It is mobile, rugged, and efficient. These attributes, though of value to the cabinetmaker, are

Safety first
The safety rules for woodworking can be condensed into one simple statement: Treat your tools with understanding and respect. Always bear in mind that tools can cut, pierce, and puncture the body as easily as they can a piece of wood. Never use a tool improperly or carelessly, and always take the time necessary to set up your work very carefully.

In any sort of a workshop, caution and common sense go a long way toward preventing accidents. In addition:
☐ Be sure you understand the function of each tool and the way it is supposed to be used before you operate it, especially when working with power tools.
☐ Read all instructions carefully; practice and proceed slowly.
☐ Don't be afraid of tools. If used correctly, they'll do your bidding.
☐ Pay close attention to what you're doing. A slip in concentration can result in a slip of a board, or a tool, or even a hand.
☐ Keep your work place neat and dry. A messy workshop easily becomes a series of booby traps that cause unnecessary accidents.
☐ Be sure to unplug electric tools when they are not in use or when you are changing the bits or blades. Always use double-insulated plugs, proper wiring, and appropriate extension cords.
☐ Keep cords out of the path of blades or drill bits.
☐ Most high-speed operations, such as cutting with a radial arm saw, produce both chips and noise. Safety glasses and hearing protectors will guard against these hazards, and, almost as important, they will increase your level of concentration.

perhaps less important than precision and versatility. So, if cabinetry is the main concern, consider a saber saw rather than a circular saw. In order to make a straight cut with either saw, clamp a guide board to the work.

The saber saw can be fitted with a variety of blades, each designed to perform a particular task. Blades are available for fine cutting in wood, cutting metal, and even cutting right up to a vertical surface. Choose a saw with variable speeds; note that some models can provide a slight orbital motion of the blade to make cleaner straight cuts. A saber saw can cut irregular shapes and with a simple attachment, can cut perfect circles.

Stationary power tools

If a lot of woodworking is done or planned, you may wish to add the following stationary power tools to your collection.

Table saw

A table saw easily cuts large pieces such as full-size sheets of plywood or particleboard. It's especially good for ripping—making a long cut in the direction of the grain to narrow a board—but it will also make crosscuts (across the grain), angle cuts, and grooves.

The saw is mounted in a fixed position, and the stock is fed past the spinning blade, which cuts the wood from underneath.

Because the wood is fed through the saw, it must be set up to allow plenty of work space behind, as well as in front of, the table.

Radial arm saw

This tool performs the same functions as a table saw. However, the blade is drawn across the wood, which means the saw can be set up against a wall rather than in the middle of the floor.

This makes a radial arm saw a more practical choice for a home workshop with limited space.

A radial arm saw has a circular blade mounted on a track to an overhead arm. To make a cut, the board is placed on the table, and the blade is drawn across the wood. The blade can be turned or tilted to make rip and bevel cuts.

Accessories such as dado blades and sanding disks are available for both table and radial arm saws.

Drill press

A drill press makes it easier to accurately drill holes of various sizes and at different angles. A variety of attachments allow it to do other jobs, such as sanding, routing, and cutting larger holes.

A less expensive alternative to buying a drill press is to buy a stand on which can be mounted, or an attachment that can be fastened to, an electric drill. These offer some of the advantages (but not the stability) of a regular drill press.

You can make elaborate pediments by buying lengths of ready-made molding. But molding can be expensive, especially when you are combining several lengths in order to create a substantial effect. An alternative is to use a router to form your own moldings. This way you can make them in a wood that matches the case.

HARDWARE

Hardware stores stock a fascinating array of small objects for woodworking. Some you'll need for your project, others aren't necessary but can enhance the design and give it a personal touch. While you're shopping, examine the full range and be imaginative when thinking about the ways these items might be put to use.

There are several different ways to fasten two pieces of wood together or to fasten a finished case to the wall. The options include the following.

Nails

Nails are the most basic type of fastener for holding two pieces of wood together. There are many types. Most of the obscure ones are for specialized construction techniques.

Common, box, finishing, and casing nails are the nails that you're most likely to use. Common nails and box nails have flat heads; box nails are thinner. Finishing and casing nails have thin shanks and small heads so that they can be countersunk (driven below the surface of the wood). The resulting holes are then filled with putty and smoothed, making the nails invisible and giving projects a neat, finished appearance.

In cabinetry, nails are used mostly to hold glued joints while the glue dries. When used alone (without glue), nails tend to loosen, eventually resulting in cases that are wobbly and weak. Even trim strips should be glued to the case and secured with a minimum of nails, since the filled nail holes may remain slightly visible.

Nails are classified by length as well as by type. The term used is penny (d). A 2-penny (2d) nail is one inch long. Size increases by one penny for each ¼ inch of length, so that a 6d nail is 2 inches long and a 10d, 3 inches.

Screws

Wood screws have threaded shafts allowing them to bite more firmly and hold better than nails. They are a little more trouble to use since you must drill holes into which to insert them.

Screws vary by length, gauge (diameter), shape of head, and type of slot. A slotted screw has a single groove across the head. A Phillips screw has two crossed slots and requires a Phillips screwdriver to tighten it. Most carpenters prefer this type because the screwdriver is less likely to slip and gouge the wood; consequently it is safer and more convenient to use driver devices, such as the spiral ratchet screwdriver and power screwdrivers.

For the projects in this book, the flat-head screw (available with either slotted or Phillips head) will be most useful because it is the least visible. The flat head lies flush with the surface of the wood and, like the finishing nail, can be countersunk and covered. If you plan to do much cabinetry that requires screws, purchase a selection of three or four combination drill bits made especially for placing wood screws. The special bits, in one maneuver, drill the pilot hole, the shank hole, the countersink, and the counterbore.

Wall fasteners

Expansion bolts, toggle bolts, and similar devices are used as anchors when you are fastening into a plaster or a plasterboard wall between studs.

The fastener is pushed through a hole that has been drilled in the wall. The wings or sleeves on the bolts spread out and tighten against the back of the finish wall, thereby preventing the bolt from slipping out.

Plates and brackets

These small metal pieces, shaped like L's and T's and I's, are useful for reinforcing the corners of a bookcase or the points where the shelves meet the side and back walls. These fittings are manufactured as flat pieces that are screwed to the edge of the case, or as three-dimensional formed clips that slip over the joint, and are usually held in place by brads. Buy plates and brackets in steel for places where they will be hidden and in brass if you want to add a decorative touch as well as strength.

Dowels

Dowels are cylindrical rods, usually made of hardwood, ranging in diameter from ⅛ to 1 inch. They can function as pegs to reinforce a joint. If used for this purpose, choose short pieces that have been grooved or fluted. (You can buy these in packages of a dozen or so.) The grooves allow for gluing along the entire length to form a firm bond. Larger dowels are sold in lengths up to several feet and can serve as structural elements in certain types of shelves, such as wine racks.

Plugs

These short pieces of dowel in various diameters are used to fill the holes made by counterbored screws.

Plugs are also available as caps, which fill the hole and protrude above the surface. The protruding part can be rounded or flat on top.

ADHESIVES

A dhesives bond two pieces of wood, sometimes making the joint between them stronger than the wood itself. They are often used in conjunction with other fasteners, particularly with nails and dowels, which by themselves don't always have enough gripping power.

On a small project that will not be subjected to great strain or abuse, the proper screws will probably secure the joints just fine. Still, some carpenters use glue on any project that they are not planning to disassemble later.

Two basic types of adhesives are employed in woodworking: exterior glues, which are waterproof, and interior glues, which are not. In most cases, a good white or yellow glue will work well for a bookcase. White glue—the familiar, easy-to-use household glue in the plastic squeeze bottle—is a polyvinyl compound. Yellow glue is an aliphatic resin designed especially for woodworking. Usually labeled carpenter's wood glue, it resembles the white type but this yellow glue is more waterproof, more stable, and equally easy to use.

If you live in a particularly humid area, or if you are building a bookcase for a damp location such as a basement recreation room, consider using a moisture-resistant adhesive, such as resorcinol or plastic-resin glue. These adhesives are more trouble to work with, however, and the extra bother may not be worth it.

Plastic laminate is bonded to cabinetry with contact cement. Use this cement in a well-ventilated area. Coat the case and the back of the laminate, let the cement set, then join the two, applying pressure with a laminate roller or rubber mallet.

Plastic laminate is one of the most professional-looking finishes for wood not fine enough to stain. First attach fractionally oversized pieces with contact cement, then use a router with a trimmer bit to cut laminate to exact size.

JOINTS

When doing any finish carpentry work, it is essential to become proficient at making neat and strong joints.

Butt joints

When the plain edge of one board is attached to the plain edge or side of another board, the joint is called a butt joint. Boards are held together with screws, bolts, or nails and glue.

Lap joints

These are fairly simple but strong and attractive joints.

Full-lap

The overlapped board is notched deep enough to accept the entire thickness of the lapping board. Never cut the notch more than one third the thickness of the board, otherwise the joint will be weak. Instead, use a heavier board or a half-lap joint.

Half-lap

This is the same as the full-lap joint except that both boards are notched.

Butt joints

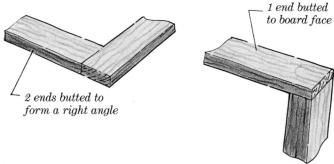

1 end butted to board face

2 ends butted to form a right angle

Half-lap joint

Full-lap joint

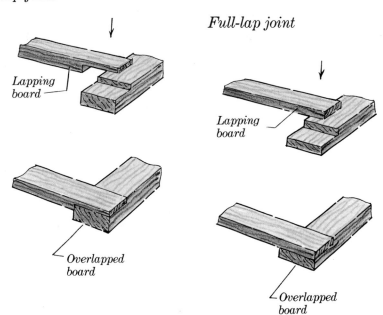

Lapping board

Lapping board

Overlapped board

Overlapped board

Cutting a lap joint with hand tools

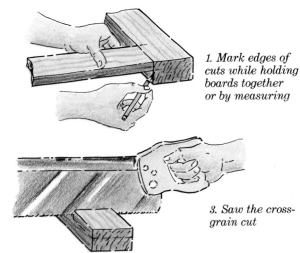

1. Mark edges of cuts while holding boards together or by measuring

2. Draw cutting lines accurately using a square

3. Saw the cross-grain cut

4. Remove the waste by sawing with the grain

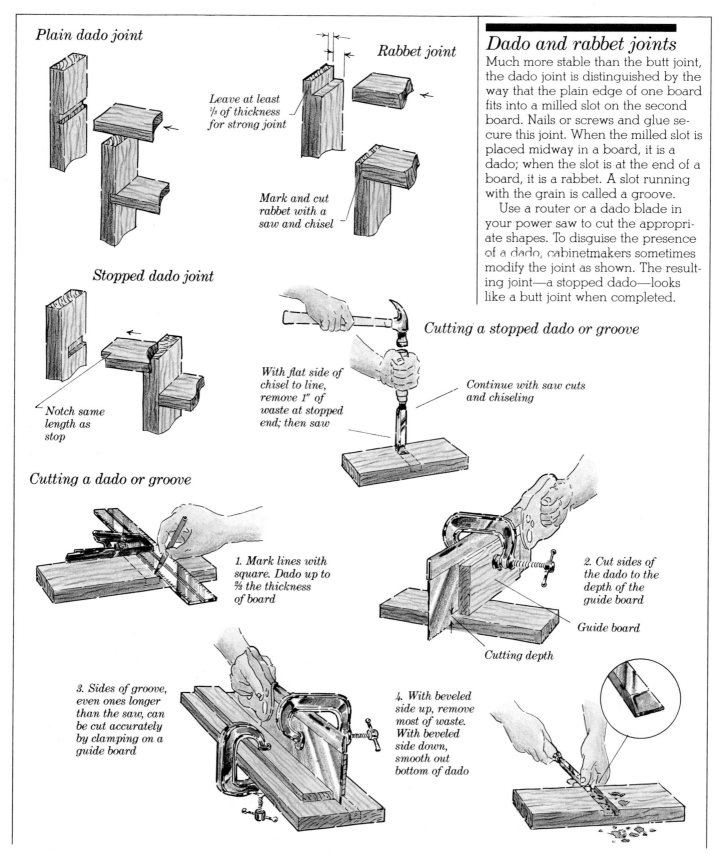

Plain dado joint

Rabbet joint

Leave at least ⅓ of thickness for strong joint

Mark and cut rabbet with a saw and chisel

Dado and rabbet joints

Much more stable than the butt joint, the dado joint is distinguished by the way that the plain edge of one board fits into a milled slot on the second board. Nails or screws and glue secure this joint. When the milled slot is placed midway in a board, it is a dado; when the slot is at the end of a board, it is a rabbet. A slot running with the grain is called a groove.

Use a router or a dado blade in your power saw to cut the appropriate shapes. To disguise the presence of a dado, cabinetmakers sometimes modify the joint as shown. The resulting joint—a stopped dado—looks like a butt joint when completed.

Stopped dado joint

Notch same length as stop

Cutting a stopped dado or groove

With flat side of chisel to line, remove 1" of waste at stopped end; then saw

Continue with saw cuts and chiseling

Cutting a dado or groove

1. Mark lines with square. Dado up to ⅔ the thickness of board

2. Cut sides of the dado to the depth of the guide board

Guide board

Cutting depth

3. Sides of groove, even ones longer than the saw, can be cut accurately by clamping on a guide board

4. With beveled side up, remove most of waste. With beveled side down, smooth out bottom of dado

25

Miter joints

This is a particularly neat way to make two pieces of wood fit together forming a right angle.

It is recommended that you cut the pieces in a miter box, although it is possible, with a lot of care, to cut a freehand miter. Strengthen these joints with glue and finishing nails, screws, or fasteners.

Doweled joints

Often these joints start out as simple butt joints, then dowels or splines are fitted into the pieces to increase strength. Always glue these joints.

If possible, drill or cut both boards at the same time to ensure that the dowels or splines will slide in easily.

Dovetail joints

True dovetails are carefully laid out and cut by hand, but a joint with a similar appearance can be created much faster using a special bit in the router and a dovetail jig.

Miter joint

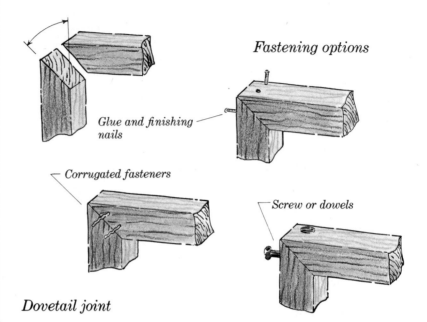

Fastening options

Glue and finishing nails

Corrugated fasteners

Screw or dowels

Dovetail joint

Dovetail template

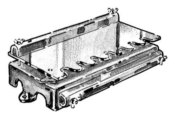

Dowel joint

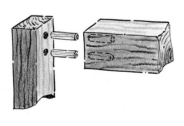

Marking dowel holes without a doweling jig

1. Hold pieces together and mark across the joint where dowels will go

2. Carry lines across edges using a square

3. Measure precisely from edges to where holes will be drilled

Mortise & tenon joint

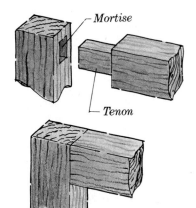

Mortise

Tenon

Tongue & groove joint

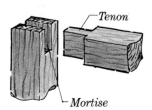

Tenon

Mortise

Mortise-and-tenon joints

When done properly, these joints are almost invisible and very strong. You must measure carefully, then chisel out the mortise and make several cuts to create the tenon.

Make the tenon first, then cut the mortise to fit. The tenon should be one third the thickness of the board cut to a depth determined by the thickness of the board that is being mortised.

Tongue-and-groove joints

These are simpler versions of the mortise-and-tenon joints but equally strong. Instead of having to cut out a mortise with a chisel, you cut a groove with a saw.

Cutting a mortise & tenon with hand tools

1. Cut the tenon first. Use a hand saw and chisel for each of these steps

2. Hold the tenon in position on the mortise and mark its outline

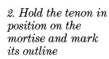

3. Drill out most of the mortise with overlapping holes. Use a piece of scrap lumber beneath to minimize splintering when drill goes through

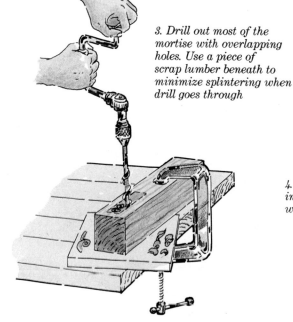

4. Finish smoothing the sides with a chisel

BUILDING TECHNIQUES

Although it is not difficult, building a case involves the same steps needed to create a more elaborate piece of furniture. The materials must be measured, then cut and shaped into individual components; the parts assembled into a structure; and the wood finished to protect it and give it color and luster. Each step is an opportunity to practice fine craftsmanship.

Customizing a case

Before finalizing your design, choose the special features that will tailor the case to your specific needs. These features include adjustable shelves, drawers, cupboard doors, or racks, in or on the case. The list is large and nearly all of the items can be incorporated into almost any of the structural designs shown in the final chapter. Because of this, the special customizing features are displayed in a chapter of their own.

Look over the "Adding Features" chapter and decide which options will best suit the case you are constructing. Make your decisions based on the look you want to achieve and the purpose and convenience of the piece. It is important to make these decisions before finalizing a design or starting construction. This way, you can adjust dimensions and make minor changes to the case. For example, if you want to hang a pair of doors on the corner cabinet shown on page 91, you will have to add a center stile to the face frame.

Construction steps

After you have designed and drawn plans for the project and have purchased materials, you are ready to begin building.

The following pointers will help you to visualize the procedure of transforming a pile of wood into an attractive and useful piece of furniture. This list is not a set of hard-and-fast rules. If the design makes it more logical to do things out of sequence, that's fine. One of the enjoyable aspects of woodworking is that there are always options.

☐ Clear your work space and check tools. Sharpen or adjust tools if necessary. Check that you have adequate supplies of such staples as glue, brads, and abrasive paper.
☐ Carefully measure and lay out the stock, then measure again.
☐ Rip boards that are not already cut to proper width.
☐ Crosscut boards to proper length.
☐ Make special cuts required by your design, such as dadoes and rabbets.
☐ Drill holes for doweled joints and shelf supports. Drill countersinks for all screw heads.
☐ Sand inside surfaces of the case as well as surfaces of shelves and dividers that will be installed inside. At this time you may want to apply a finish (stain or paint) and attach hardware to the inside surfaces.
☐ Assemble the face frame, if the design calls for one, and let glue set.
☐ Assemble the case, joining sides (and vertical dividers, if any) to top and bottom pieces. Set in any fixed shelves, and attach a face frame and the back panel.
☐ Measure the interior and openings of assembled case.
☐ Lay out and cut movable shelf boards and drawer pieces.
☐ Cut grooves, dadoes, and rabbets on drawer pieces.
☐ Assemble the drawers, insert and check them for proper fit, then remove for finishing.
☐ Lay out and cut the cabinet doors. Assemble door pieces, if necessary. Check for fit, but do not install yet.
☐ Fill or plug any nail and screw holes that might possibly show. Fill cracks and imperfections.
☐ Rough-sand entire project, wiping away dust when finished. Remember that a scraper can be used in place of abrasive paper. Reinspect the piece and fill any remaining flaws.
☐ Apply a sanding sealer (unless it conflicts with the finish you have selected) then sand entire project with finer abrasive paper.
☐ Apply the finish of your choice. See page 33 for finish alternatives. Sand project or rub with steel wool, and apply another coat of finish. Repeat these finishing steps, if required.
☐ Install shelf brackets, hang shelves, hang cabinet doors, and install drawers. Adjust drawer glides and door hinges so that they operate smoothly.
☐ Fit latches, pulls, and special hardware, if any.

When you build your own cases you can
size sections to suit the equipment that
they will store. Here, shelf space at the
top matches the height of the speaker,
and the lower shelves are deeper so that
records don't overhang the edge.

Preparing a work space

Clean up your work space and check your tools. Make sure saw blades, chisels, and drill bits are sharp. Unless you have special sharpening equipment, take saws and drill bits to a professional sharpener (look in the Yellow Pages). Chisels and plane blades can be sharpened on a whetstone, using a simple plastic jig that holds blades at the proper angle during sharpening. Check and repair worn or damaged electrical cords.

Measuring and cutting

When measuring and cutting material, be as efficient as possible. Minimize waste, or at least try to keep leftover pieces large enough to be useful for a future project. Plan the pieces so that the grain of the wood always runs in the same direction—one cabinet door shouldn't have a vertical-grain pattern and another, a horizontal pattern. On shelves, keep in mind that the grain should run lengthwise in order for it to have adequate strength.

If you lack extensive experience, initially cut only the material needed for the main structural parts of the cabinet, leaving the back panel, dividers, shelves, drawers, and doors until later. That way you can take measurements from the assembled cabinet and avoid mistakes.

Experienced cabinetmakers scribe measurements onto wood with sharp tools. Purchase a scribe and marking

Even if your case is designed to look like a homemade country piece rather than a sophisticated period reproduction, take the time and care necessary to make sure that it doesn't appear amateurishly built.

gauge or simply use a sharp pencil. Most importantly, when cutting material, make the cut on the waste side of the scribed line or mark, preserving the mark on the board.

When cutting dadoes, rabbets, grooves, and mortises, always use scrap wood to set up tools. Don't cut actual material until all adjustments on equipment have been made.

After cutting but before assembling the collection of pieces, take the time to do some finishing work.

The first thing you should do is plane rough or oversized pieces, clean out mortises and dadoes with a utility knife, and generally sand all the edges and surfaces that will be hard to reach once the project is assembled. You may even want to apply finish to inside surfaces and install drawer guides or turntables on pieces that will be hard to reach once the case is assembled.

Checking the fit

When the major pieces are properly prepared, loosely assemble the case, without fasteners or glue, just to check the fit. Of course it will probably be impossible to assemble the whole case in its final form, but make sure at least that any 17-inch pieces

weren't cut to 7 inches by mistake. And, check that dadoes and mortises will accept their respective counterparts—you don't want to discover mistakes after applying glue.

Assembling the case

If the pieces fit, start the assembly. Each project demands a different order of assembly. A cabinet with H-shaped dividers might require that the dividers be assembled first, then installed as a subassembly when the rest of the case is put together. A bookcase, on the other hand, might require that you set a number of fixed shelves into one side panel and quickly fit the other side panel before all the glued joints set up. Two rules that you should always follow when assembling a case are:
☐ Carefully plan the order of assembly before starting to make sure that there is a way to install each subsequent piece.
☐ Square up and clamp the case each time you pause to let glue dry.

Applying a face frame

If the pieces that make up your case are plywood, it will be necessary to cover the exposed front edges. And, even if that case is made of solid wood, a face frame will give a professionally finished look.

A face frame is constructed from thin boards of solid wood. A similar effect can be accomplished by applying sheet or tape veneer, but if a design includes doors, it is easier to attach the hinges to a face frame.

FINISHING TECHNIQUES

Finishing provides the crowning touch, turning a raw box into a piece of furniture. The finish provides practical advantages such as protecting wood from stains, moisture, and drying out. It is also done for aesthetic reasons to bring out the grain, change the color, provide a glossy texture and sheen, and enhance the natural quality of the wood.

Filling the gaps

Even the best woodworker will find small gaps here or there that need to be filled. In addition to gaps, there will generally be nail holes (make sure all nail heads are set), imperfections in the wood, damage from handling or accident, and saw holes (counterbores) to fill.

There are several types of tinted wood filler available in stores, including acetone-based putty, oil-based crayons, and latex paste. To decide which type to use, read the various labels. Or better, solicit the advice of a salesperson after describing the wood, the nature of the filling to be done, and the type of finish you plan to use. If you are planning to paint the project, you can choose from a wide range of fillers. When using a clear finish or stain, both the color and the absorptive qualities of the wood must be considered.

Apply filler with a flat tool that will force the filler into the void, then will scrape away the excess. Large gaps or gouges will often require more than one application since many of the filler materials shrink as they dry.

Sanding

Most finishes immediately draw the eye to any flaws in the surface of the wood. Even paint won't hide dents and gouges. The amount of time spent sanding, cleaning, and repairing the surface will be rewarded by the high-quality appearance of the finished piece.

Sanding is a three-stage process. The first stage, part of the cleanup and repair process, requires sanding with rough (80-grit) abrasive paper. The second stage is to smooth with 120-grit or 180-grit paper. Do the last stage after sealing the case: This is to sand once more with very fine-grained paper (220-grit, or even 400-grit if using a finish such as lacquer that needs an extremely smooth surface).

Electric sanders can be very helpful in the first two stages of this process, but they leave oscillation marks or slight gouges. Many carpenters prefer to do the final sanding by hand because they can remove these flaws and do more exacting work. Make sure the final sanding is done with, not against, the grain.

When properly sharpened, a cabinet scraper performs the same function as rough abrasive paper, leaving the finish of fine paper.

Sealing

Some carpenters like to use sealers to close the pores in the wood, smooth the surface, and reduce the absorbency. A sealer also helps wood take stain or paint more evenly, thus making the final finish easier to apply.

Sealer can also be used as an intermediary coat between the stain and the final finish. This prevents the two substances from bleeding into each other. (Occasionally a stain reacts to the finish and oozes into it.) Using just a sealer can be an adequate finish for a particleboard case in a garage or utility room.

Staining

Stains add color to the wood while showing off the natural grain. With one exception (penetrating oil stains), they don't protect the wood. You still need a top coat of shellac, varnish, or wax. Test the color on a scrap of wood to make sure you like the result.

Water-based stains. These dyes are very clear and come in brilliant colors. They penetrate wood evenly, are easy to clean up, and are very safe to use. The main drawback is that they tend to raise the grain of the wood, lifting the individual fibers and making the surface rough and furry. This will mean extra sanding before you apply the finish coat.

Pigmented oil stains. These are widely used, easy to apply, and come in a wide range of colors. They tend to be darker and more opaque than water-based stains and can bleed into the surface finish if left unsealed.

Alcohol or spirit stains. These stains don't bleed or raise the grain, but aren't as colorfast as other types. They dry very rapidly and are often applied with a spray.

Penetrating oil stains. This is the one type of stain that can be used as a final finish. However, the furniture will benefit from the extra protection and luster provided by a coat of wax. Penetrating oil stains can be found on the hardware store shelf labeled tung oil or Danish oil. They soak into the wood, sealing it rather than just coating it, but still allowing the texture of the natural wood to show through.

Final finishing

The final finish adds smoothness, sheen, and sometimes color to a case. It protects the wood and keeps it looking good for a long time.

Varnish, shellac, lacquer, plastic finishes such as polyurethane, wax, oils, and, of course, paint, are among the many types of finish options. The choice depends on the material and the look you desire. The chart, opposite, compares the principal types.

Finishing materials

	Description	Use	Application	Comments
Paint (gloss-finish enamel)	An opaque, usually oil- or synthetic-based, liquid that dries to a hard finish	For coloring and protecting wood	Brush, spray	Wood must be sealed or primed. Apply 2 or more coats. Sand with abrasive paper or steel wool between coats
Varnish	Clear wood finish. New synthetic varnishes are generally superior to traditional formulations	For enhancing appearance of and protecting wood	Brush, spray	A durable finish that shows off the depth and grain pattern of the wood; resists moisture, including alcoholic beverages. Fairly slow drying
Shellac	Clear to slightly cloudy	To protect raw or stained wood or as a sanding sealer or sealer under stain or paint	Brush or spray	Similar protective and visual qualities as varnish, but much faster drying. Clean up with ammonia and warm water (or alcohol)
Lacquer	Clear protective wood finish	Very workable finish for fine furniture pieces	Spray. Apply 3 coats rubbing with steel wool between coats. Leave final coat glossy or rub to a satin finish	Use a wood filler to create a smooth base for lacquer finish; very fast drying time simplifies application of multiple coats
Water-based stains	Powder or premixed liquid. Well suited to enhancing the grain of premium hardwoods	For tinting wood	Rag, brush, or spray. Dampen wood first	These are stains designed to be used under a protective clear finish
Pigmented oil stain	Premixed liquid	For tinting wood	Apply with brush or cloth; wipe off excess	Well suited for darker tints on softwoods. When dry, apply a clear finish for protection
Alcohol or spirit stain	Powder or premixed liquid	Mostly commercial. Use a fine spray for shading	Spray	Use in spray applicator for shading and refinishing
Penetrating oil stain	Linseed or tung oil–based premixed liquid	Tinting and protecting wood	Brush, cloth	Apply paste wax for added luster and protection
Wax	Paste compound that dries to a hard, lustrous finish	To protect oiled finishes and for added protection	Apply with a rag. Buff with a clean rag	A wax finish over penetrating oil stain gives a warm, lustrous appearance
Oil	Ranges from translucent to dark-tinted liquid (linseed or tung oil)	To color wood and give it a hard(er) surface	Brush on; wipe off with rag	Soaks into the wood giving a warm, lustrous appearance

ADDING FEATURES

Y ou've planned where the case is going to go; you've decided on basic proportions and have selected the material; now it's time to choose the special features.

These features will make the case look distinctive and function conveniently. Shelves can be fixed or adjustable. Doors can be flush, paneled, bifold, or sliding. The following pages present ideas and many alternatives to individualize the case and make it suitable for your storage needs.

Flip back and forth between this chapter and the one that follows to select the options, the case, and the look you want to create.

When bookcases are built to exact dimensions they become an integral part of a wall. Here, face frames match the height of the mirrored fireplace wall.

SHELVES

*S*helves are the one element found in all bookcases and in most cabinets. Although simple in concept, they deserve some forethought and planning.

When planning a case intended for storage, measure the items you want to accommodate. It may not bother you that the record albums (12½ inches square) will stick out beyond the edge of an 11½-inch shelf, but you should know this will happen before you build.

Strength

The weight that the shelf will carry is a critical factor in the design. A set of encyclopedias puts a far greater strain on a shelf than a dozen paperbacks. An overloaded shelf is not likely to break, but it will sag and destroy the aesthetics of the case, giving it an appearance of instability.

Increasing the strength

You can increase the load-bearing capacity of a shelf in any one of a number of ways.

☐ Use solid wood; it's more rigid than plywood. Particleboard can snap under too much weight.
☐ Install fixed shelves rather than adjustable ones. If shelves are tied into the structure of a case, they will be stronger.
☐ Reinforce the points where the fixed shelf meets the sides and back of the case with wood cleats or metal brackets.
☐ Trim the edge of the shelf with a continuous strip of lumber.
☐ Make the shelf thicker. The thicker the lumber, the stronger the shelf.
☐ Make the shelf shorter. The greater the span, the weaker the shelf. Even a strong shelf tends to sag under the weight of a full load of books or

records if it is more than about 30 inches long.
☐ Sandwich 1 by 2s or 2 by 4s between two pieces of plywood or particleboard.

Quick shelf assembly

The one element that all quick shelving units have in common is shelf and side panels of the same width. Whether you use 1 by 10, 1 by 12, or 12-inch-wide strips of plywood, you need only cut the pieces to the proper length to create the unit.

Shelf boards

The illustrations shown represent variations on a simple theme. The 2-by shelf is naturally stronger than the 1-by shelf, all else being equal. But the strength of a 1-by shelf can be increased somewhat by gluing and nailing 1 by 2 boards to the front and back edges. Of course, if the back of the shelf will be supported by a ledger board or cleat, or by clips or brackets, then there is no need to attach a reinforcing board across the back edge. To gain even more strength, and without the added weight of 2-by boards, build a composite shelf with top and bottom layers of tempered hardboard or lightweight plywood glued and nailed to a framework of milled or plain 1 by 2 or 2 by 2 stock.

Appearance

Improve the appearance of the shelves by routing a decorative edge on the front of each shelf board. If you don't have a router, or if you want to cover the edge of plywood or particleboard shelving, simply affix wood tape veneer to the edges of the shelf board, or glue on strips of wood veneer. For a shaped edge, glue and nail on a strip of molding. A number of appropriate moldings are available, including ogee-shaped ones as well as the simple half-round type.

Shelf options

2-by shelf, plain

1-by shelf, plain

1x2s added to 1-by for strength

Strong, lightweight shelves with milled structural edges

Milled edge on front

Molding attached to front edge

Fixed shelves

In order for a case to have structural integrity, plan on including at least two fixed shelves—one at the bottom and one placed approximately half-way up. If flexibility of shelf positions is not a major consideration, the case will be stronger if there are more than two fixed shelves.

Cleats

Whether adding shelves to a niche, a built-in cabinet, or a movable case, the simplest, most economical approach is to attach plain cleats to the inner sides of the storage area, and set the shelf boards directly on them. Unless you attach the shelving to the cleats, they are not really fixed shelves, but you can't change the location of the shelves without changing the location of the cleats (or adding new ones).

Don't reject the idea of cleats merely because you don't like the way they look. Realize that a cleat can be placed relatively inconspicuously under the back edge of a shelf where the support will greatly reduce the chances of a shelf sagging in the middle. You can also rout a pattern into the visible edges of the cleats to improve the appearance.

Dadoes

A freestanding bookcase will be much stronger if the shelves are dadoed into the sides of the case. This joint will also make the shelves a bit stronger.

Make the dado as wide as the shelf is thick, and as deep as one half of the thickness of the shelf (but never cut it more than halfway through the side panel). Because the shelf boards will fit tightly into the dadoes, set in the shelves as you assemble the outer portion of the case. Be sure to have a rubber mallet on hand to use during assembly. Apply glue in the dado, and drive finishing nails through from the outside to secure the shelves.

The front edges of shelves set into dadoes are not particularly attractive.

These joints can be covered by attaching strips of lattice or molding along the edges of the side panels.

Stopped dadoes

An alternative version of the dado joint is called a stopped dado. This eliminates the need for trim strips.

This joint is appropriate for a simple bookcase design or for a clean, Scandinavian-style design where trim is kept to a minimum. The stopped dado and other joints are described on pages 24–27.

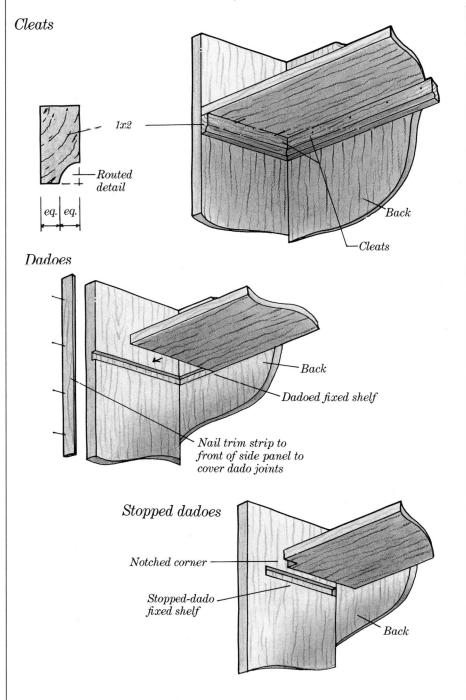

Cleats

1x2

Routed detail

eq. | eq.

Back

Cleats

Dadoes

Back

Dadoed fixed shelf

Nail trim strip to front of side panel to cover dado joints

Stopped dadoes

Notched corner

Stopped-dado fixed shelf

Back

Adjustable shelves

Many methods have been devised over the years for supporting shelves in a way that allows for adjustment.

Notched standards

A traditional method is to use cleats as notched standards. Although not difficult to construct, this support system does require precision cutting that will take time.

The system consists of four notched standards mounted in the four corners of the case. The ends of the cleats (two for each shelf) are cut on an angle to match the notches, and support the shelf at any height.

Using 1 by 2 stock, construct 4 standards and 2 cleats for each shelf. Make the notches by cutting 30/60 degree triangles as shown. If your equipment will handle it, cut 2 or more standards at the same time. Cut cleats with corresponding angles (see illustration) to the desired length (the depth between the front and back standard). Notch the corner of each shelf to allow clearance for the notched standards.

In a bookcase with multiple bays, add cleats and standards at intermediary points to support continuous shelves. Cover fronts of standards with a face frame or trim strips.

Pegs

A more straightforward way to support adjustable shelves is to drill into (but not through) the inner sides of the case, insert dowel pegs into the holes, and lay shelves on the pegs.

Use ¼-inch-diameter, or larger, dowels and space holes every 2 inches or so. Lay out the boards carefully before drilling; misaligned holes will result in crooked shelves. Use a drill guide and a collar stop on the drill bit to ensure that you don't drill through the side panels.

Clips

A contemporary version of the hole-and-dowel system substitutes L-shaped metal clips held in the holes by attached pins.

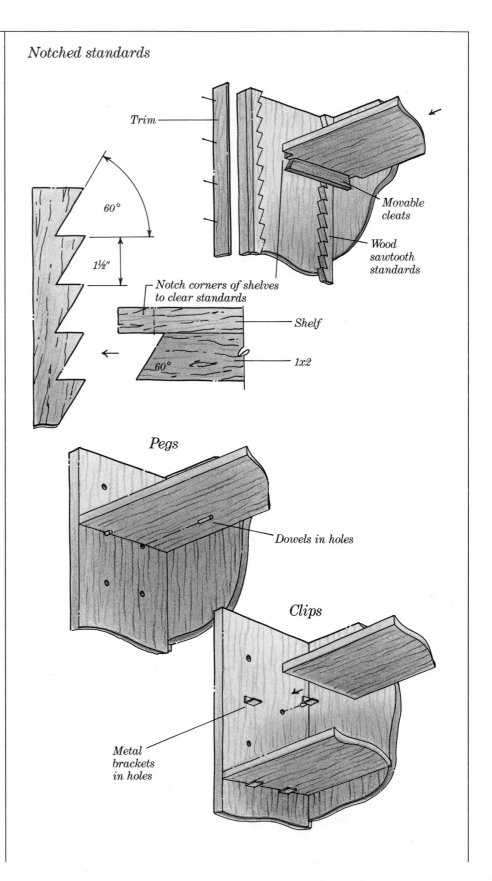

Notched standards

Trim

60°

1½"

60°

Notch corners of shelves to clear standards

Movable cleats

Wood sawtooth standards

Shelf

1x2

Pegs

Dowels in holes

Clips

Metal brackets in holes

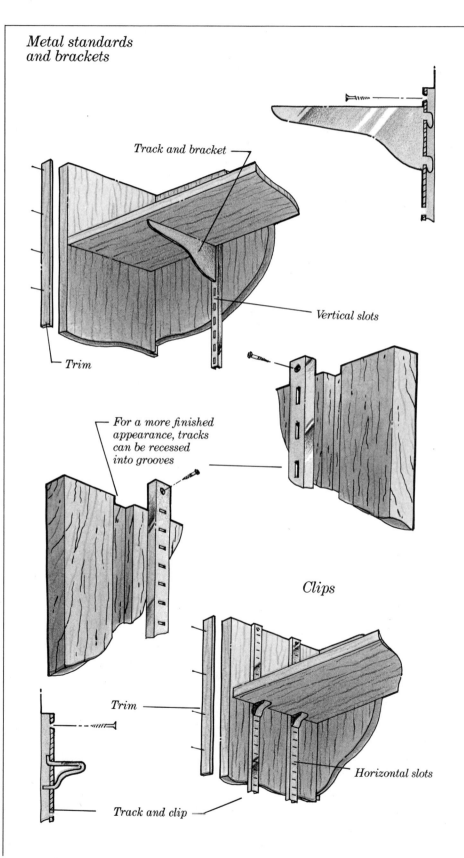

Metal standards and brackets

Track and bracket

Vertical slots

Trim

For a more finished appearance, tracks can be recessed into grooves

Clips

Trim

Horizontal slots

Track and clip

Metal standards

Track systems for supporting shelves are the most common way of mounting adjustable shelves. By fastening standards directly to a wall and clipping on support brackets, it is possible to turn nearly any wall into a library or storage area. These standards, available in a variety of finishes including silver, gold, bronze, black, and white, allow you to position shelves in a variety of heights and are quick and easy to install.

Use the vertically slotted standards and brackets for shelves with a long span or for shelves that will carry a good deal of weight. Purchase brackets that correspond to the width of the shelf boards. Keep in mind that because the vertically slotted standards attach to the back panel of your case, you must use material for the back panel that is strong enough to support the shelf system. This system works well where a cabinet is built into a wall niche and the standards can be anchored into studs in the rear wall.

In situations where the shelf span is shorter or the load lighter, use the horizontally slotted standards and clips. Install a pair of standards vertically on the inside face of each side wall to support the ends of the shelves. Intermediate standards can be installed in the backs of cases that have one or more vertical dividers in the face frame. Since these intermediary standards are set at right angles to the end standards, the shelf boards must be made narrower or notched to accommodate them.

The appearance of either track system is improved when the standards are recessed into grooves cut or routed into the panels to which they are attached. This is particularly true of the horizontally slotted standards. The brackets used in the vertically slotted system have deeper tangs, which require deeper standards and, consequently, deeper grooves. Before starting construction, make sure the case material is thick enough to accept a deep groove.

Connectors

Manufactured in L, T, and X shapes, shelf connectors are designed to clip together 1-by boards. Each connector is predrilled with several small holes through which nails or screws are driven into shelf boards.

Clips are available in either plastic or metal in a limited number of colors and finishes. They can, of course, be easily spray-painted any color. When buying connectors, remember to get enough to fasten both front and back faces of the unit.

Using shelf connectors, you can build a freestanding shelf unit or one sized to fit into a cabinet. The look, though rather informal, is suitable for a laundry room or workshop. Or, the connectors can be emphasized by spray-painting them with bright-colored enamel, in one or more colors to make a high-tech statement. Because a cabinet built with clips can be disassembled without too much trouble, this system is particularly appropriate for informal furniture in a dormitory or apartment.

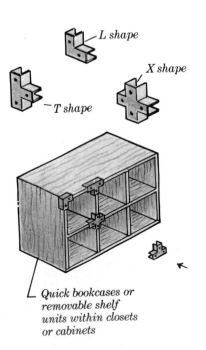

L shape

X shape

T shape

Quick bookcases or removable shelf units within closets or cabinets

Wood-block connectors

Create your own shelf connectors out of wood. This simple shelf system will please the youngsters in the family. It is inexpensive and easy to make, can be painted a bright color, and invites youngsters' participation—at least during the final assembly.

Make 10-inch-square units using vertical-grain fir 2 by 2s for the blocks and ¼-inch tempered hardboard for the panels. The size of the case depends on the number of units built. After painting, glue blocks and panels together, scraping away paint as necessary to get a good bond.

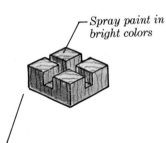

Spray paint in bright colors

Create your own connectors on a table saw. Use sections of 2x2 vertical grain fir with ¾" slots for tempered, solid or perforated hardboard. Glue together

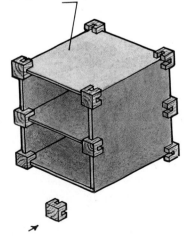

Metal brackets

The following metal brackets can be found in most hardware stores.

Metal angles

Formed out of flat steel, these brackets are available in L and T shapes.

Use them with 2-by boards to build sturdy shelves that will hold heavy items. Select ¾-inch-wide or larger brackets for 2-by shelving. Secure them to studs, then to shelves, using flat-head wood screws.

Shelf brackets

Shelves can be mounted quickly using metal shelf brackets. These are widely available, usually in gray, in several sizes corresponding to the standard dimensions of shelf boards.

For best results, screw brackets into the wall at points where studs are located. The result is shelving suitable for light, bulky items; too much weight will cause shelves to tip down.

Closet shelf brackets

This variation on the plain shelf bracket is designed to support a closet shelf and a pole on which to hang clothes. Because clothes on hangers make a particularly heavy load, this type of bracket is fitted with a welded support bar.

These brackets can also be used in a garage for shelves that hold heavy objects. Screw brackets into the wall at stud locations. As an added feature, two appropriately placed brackets can store a bicycle.

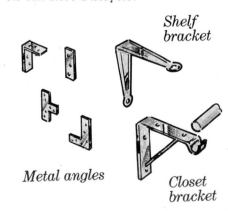

Shelf bracket

Metal angles

Closet bracket

FLOATING SHELVES

For dramatic visual appeal and to make shelves that appear to be cantilevered straight out from the wall, you can support them on pegs. The pegs are screwed into studs in the wall.

However, there are a few things to consider before you decide that this is the project for you.

☐ Don't use this system if you plan to load shelves with heavy items. The primary appeal is visual, not utilitarian. Use this hanging method for shelves that will hold framed pictures, flower arrangements, objets d'art, mementos, and maybe a few small- to medium-sized books.

☐ Since the pegs attach to the studs that frame the wall, you need to locate the studs and determine that their placement is suitable for the peg locations. Studs are usually, but not always, spaced at 16-inch intervals, so do some checking. Hardware stores sell stud finders, but if the walls are smooth plasterboard, the locations of nails or screws can usually be found by shining a flashlight beam parallel to the wall surface.

☐ When drilling pilot holes into the wall studs, it is very important to avoid drilling into any electrical wires within the wall. Driving a nail into a wire usually results in a short circuit and tripped breaker, but could cause a fire. Drilling into a wire can electrocute you. Be absolutely sure that you have located any electrical wires in the wall, and never drill too close to them. As an extra precaution, turn off the appropriate circuit.

Building the shelves

To build shelves on pegs, first plot out the location(s) on the wall. Next, assemble the materials. Using 1 by 8 stock, cut shelf boards approximately 8 inches longer than the distance between the 2 end pegs.

Making the pegs

Calculate the number of pegs needed (each shelf needs 1 in each stud) and buy enough 1 1/4-inch-diameter closet pole to yield the correct number of 7 1/4-long pegs. Buy the same number of 5/16-inch-diameter by 8-inch-long lag screws as you have pegs, with end caps of your choosing (see illustration). You can make your own end caps—in a diamond shape for instance—by cutting them from scrap shelf board or plywood.

Drill 5/16-inch-diameter holes 3 inches into the wall at the stud locations. Use a level to make sure the holes line up with each other. Also use a drill guide to ensure that the holes are all exactly 3 inches deep and perpendicular to the wall.

Insert a lag screw into each hole so that it protrudes 5 inches (not counting the head). Cut off head of each screw with a hacksaw. Alternatively, you can cut off the heads first and use a small pipe wrench to attach screws to the wall.

Using a drill press with the table turned sideways, clamp each peg to the table and drill a 5/16-inch-diameter hole 5 1/2 inches into the end of the peg. If you don't have a drill press, make a bench top jig to hold the pegs, and drill holes by sliding an electric drill along the bench top. In either case, take care to make the holes straight and centered in the pegs. Glue an end cap onto the nondrilled end of each peg.

When glue is dry, sand and paint pegs and shelf boards. Slide pegs onto lag screws and set shelf boards in place.

If a peg fails to fit snugly, wrap some tape on the shaft of the lag screw. Or, drip a little glue into the drilled hole, let it dry overnight, then slide peg over the lag screw.

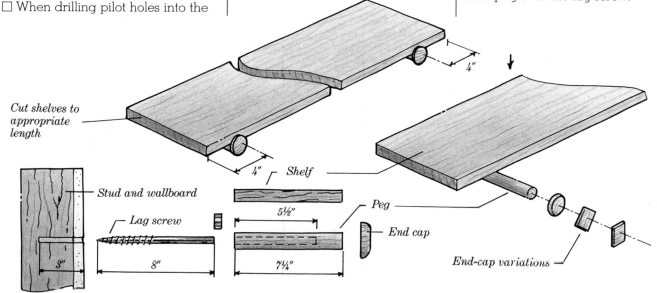

Cut shelves to appropriate length

4"

4"

Shelf

Stud and wallboard

Lag screw

3"

8"

5½"

7¼"

Peg

End cap

End-cap variations

*I*t is a good idea to put doors on cases whenever the stored items need to be protected from dust or hidden from view.

The basic construction for a case with doors need not be substantially different from a bookcase, so what follows is a discussion about the doors themselves. After deciding on a basic case design, you might choose to enclose just part of the case with doors and leave the rest as open shelving. Look over the possibilities illustrated on the following pages.

Flush doors

The term flush door has a double meaning in cabinetry terminology. First, it describes a door that has a flat front surface as opposed to a door with a raised panel. The door can be made from a sheet of plywood with a paint or varnish finish, or it can be surfaced with veneer or plastic laminate. But whatever the material, the surface is flat.

The second meaning of the term flush refers to the way in which the door panel is mounted onto the cabinet. As you might expect, the front of a flush door is in the same plane as the front of the cabinet. This means that the door has to be small enough to fit within the opening, and special consideration has to be given to the way in which the door is hinged.

Making flush doors

Plywood is most commonly used for making flush doors. For economy, particleboard will suffice for flush door panels in a garage or workshop.

Finishing flush doors

Plywood is easy to paint. For installations where a wood finish is desired, you can get a grade where the surfaces are hardwood veneers and finish them with varnish. Whenever a finished appearance is called for, remember to finish the edges of the door. Always finish both sides of a door with similar materials; if one side absorbs more moisture than the other side, the panel will warp.

There are several alternatives to paint or varnish worth considering if you are looking for a fancier or more durable finish. Note that these suggestions do not apply to lipped doors.

Plastic Laminate. Affixing sheets of plastic laminate will increase the durability and moisture resistance of door panels. Remember that both sides of the door should be covered to prevent warping.

Start with the side edges: Cut strips of laminate that are fractionally wider than the doors are thick and long enough to avoid joint. Glue strips to both side edges with contact cement. When cement has set, trim off excess with a laminate-trimmer bit placed in a router. Cover top and bottom edges following the same procedure.

When all 4 edges are covered, cut a panel fractionally larger than the door. Glue it to the front surface, let it dry, then trim. Repeat procedure for back surface.

Veneer. You can dress up plain plywood doors by applying good-looking, wood veneer. To surface plywood with veneer, follow exactly the same procedure as described above for applying plastic laminate.

Emulating paneled doors. Rather than a finish, this is a different look. If you want to dress up the appearance of flush doors to make them fit in with a traditional decor, you can nail and glue small moldings to the fronts of the doors to mimic the look of a paneled door.

Use a rectangular pattern, or a pattern of several rectangles, cutting 45-degree miters at the corners of the molding. Unless you can match the molding stock to the wood used for the fronts of the door panels, this approach works best on doors that will be painted. Of course, with the molding attached, the doors are no longer true flush doors.

Mounting flush doors

Flush doors can be surface-mounted on a cabinet, that is, mounted so they overlap the door openings. They can be partially inset, as in the case of lipped doors; or they can be flush-mounted, meaning that they are inset into the door openings.

Making doors flush

Cabinet designs that call for doors mounted flush often call for flush-type doors, as well. If this seems confusing, read Flush Doors, at right. What follows deals with the mounting of doors onto a cabinet structure in a way referred to as flush—meaning that the front surfaces of the doors are in the same plane as the front of the cabinet.

If possible, build the cabinet structure first, making it as square and plumb as you can. Then take measurements for the inset (flush) doors directly from the openings in the case. Creating doors that hang so there is an equal amount of space on each of the four sides will be a test of your cabinetmaking skills, or at least good practice!

Cut door panels 3/16 inch shorter and narrower than the openings in the case; this will result in a 3/32-inch gap around each door. If you plan to apply either plastic laminate or veneer to the case or the door panels, remember to subtract the appropriate number of added thicknesses from the door measurements. Additionally, cut the latch edge of flush doors at a slight inward bevel—approximately 5 degrees—to allow adequate clearance when they are opened. This is particularly critical on narrow doors or doors of thick material.

Hinges for flush doors

A variety of hardware is manufactured for hinging flush-mounted doors to a case.

Butt hinges. The most common is the universal butt hinge, widely available in hardware stores in several finishes and many sizes. Pick the size equal to the thickness of your door panel or face frame, whichever is smaller. To maintain an even gap around the door panel, mortise one or both of the hinge leaves into the door edge and/or face frame.

A special hinge with a right-angle bend in one of the leaves allows you to attach the hinge to the back of the door. This type is recommended if you are using particleboard. Note that the pivot portion of the hinge will be visible on the finished case. This may not bother you; if it does, consider other options.

Pivot hinges. The pivot-type hidden hinge attaches at the top and bottom edges of the door. It requires some mortising and is not entirely hidden. Other versions of the pivot hidden hinge are designed to be mounted middoor, with the pivot protruding through a small kerf in the edge of the door.

Invisible hinges. Several types of completely invisible hinges are available for flush-mounted doors. (They are not invisible when the door is open, however!) One type attaches to the inside of the storage area and to the backside of the door panel. Another type fits into bores made in the edge of the face frame and the edge of the door panel. Check local hardware and home-center stores to see what is available in your area.

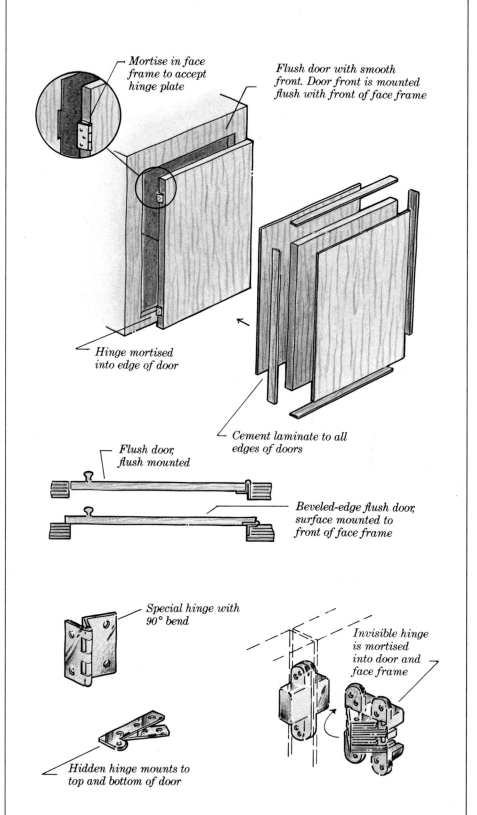

Mortise in face frame to accept hinge plate

Flush door with smooth front. Door front is mounted flush with front of face frame

Hinge mortised into edge of door

Cement laminate to all edges of doors

Flush door, flush mounted

Beveled-edge flush door, surface mounted to front of face frame

Special hinge with 90° bend

Invisible hinge is mortised into door and face frame

Hidden hinge mounts to top and bottom of door

43

Cabinets will stay much tidier if they are fitted to suit the contents. In a kitchen slide-out shelves allow convenient and easy access to large cooking utensils.

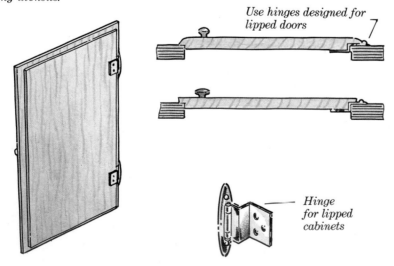

Use hinges designed for lipped doors

Hinge for lipped cabinets

Lipped doors

Flush-mounted doors are mounted within the openings in the face frame; surface-mounted doors are mounted on top of the openings. Lipped doors can be described as a combination of those two types of door-mounting techniques. This results in the advantages of the relatively forgiving fit requirements of the surface-mounted door as well as the sleeker, or at least slimmed-down, appearance of the flush-mounted door.

The lipped door requires both a unique door construction and a special mounting technique.

Making lipped doors

Make each door panel ½-inch taller and ⅝ inch wider than its respective opening. If you want the outer edges of the door panel to be rounded (a common practice with lipped door panels), rout the edges now using a ¼-inch radius bit.

Whether the doors are made from ¾-inch sheet stock (such as birch plywood), or are built in a paneled style (see Paneled Doors, opposite), the next step in fitting them is to cut the rabbets at the door edges. Rout or cut a ⅜-inch by ⅜-inch rabbet along all 4 inner edges of each door.

Hanging lipped doors

Purchase ⅜-inch offset lipped door hinges, and mount the doors. The hinges are available in regular or self-closing versions, but there is no type of hidden hinge for a lipped door.

When building a cabinet that will contain lipped doors, remember to use face-frame members wide enough to allow sufficient clearance for lips and hinges.

Paneled doors

Building paneled doors is challenging, but the results can be gratifying. An exploded view of paneled-door construction is shown below. However, it is advisable to follow any instructions that may accompany your router set or shaper bits. Note that at least three bits are required: one to rout grooves in stiles and rails; one to mate stiles to rails; and one to taper edges of panels. Paneled doors are normally rabbeted at the edges so that they can be partially inset into the cabinet openings.

There are many variations on the paneled door. By modifying any number of moldings sold at lumberyards, you can create frames into which any rigid sheet material can be mounted. One method calls for mounting the panel into the frame in a fashion similar to mounting a picture in a picture frame. (See Glazed-Panel Doors, below.) Another variation is the mock-paneled door, in which the appearance of panel construction is created by routing a pattern into ¾-inch board or sheet stock.

Raised-panel doors

You will recognize raised-panel doors as the most familiar of the traditional door types. Each door has one or more panels that are set into a frame composed of vertical stiles and horizontal rails. If you choose to make this type of door for your cabinet project, you will need a heavy-duty router and router table, or a shaper, and special sets of panel-door bits to use in your machine. Assembling the doors will be easier if you have, or make, a gluing table with a large flat surface and bench dogs (stops that can be inserted into holes drilled into the work surface) to be used with a wide tail vise. Bar clamps large enough to span the longest door dimension will work in place of the wide tail vise.

Glazed-panel doors

In any panel-door construction, the raised panel may be replaced with a sheet of glass, thereby putting the cabinet contents on view. The grooves routed into the stiles and rails must be open on the inside edges and will therefore be rabbets rather than grooves. Thin quarter-round molding is tacked to the inside of the rabbets to complete the grooves and hold the glass in place. If you are making panel doors to show off your leaded-glass handiwork (or perhaps you are the woodworker and your partner is the artist in glass), make sure the quarter-round is strong enough to secure the glass firmly in place. The quarter-round should also be removable so that the glass can be replaced if necessary.

Make stiles and rails thin and rectangular for a contemporary look or wider and more ornate for a more traditional look.

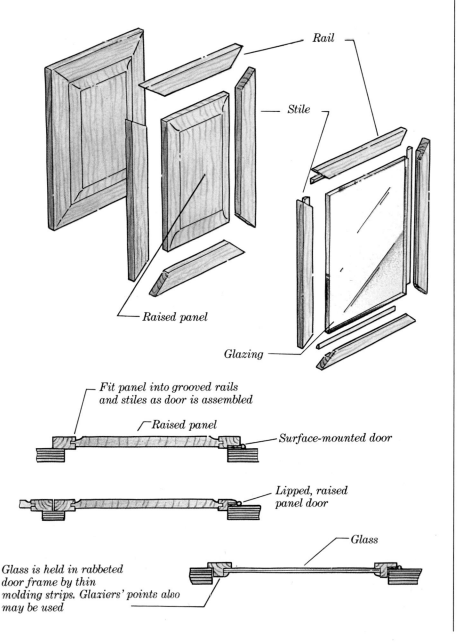

Rail

Stile

Raised panel

Glazing

Fit panel into grooved rails
and stiles as door is assembled

Raised panel

Surface-mounted door

Lipped, raised
panel door

Glass

Glass is held in rabbeted
door frame by thin
molding strips. Glaziers' points also
may be used

Bifold doors

When fitting a large cabinet into a small room or constricted area, the space required to allow the doors to swing open freely can sometimes be a problem. Bifold doors allow access to wide storage spaces without needing a large swing-out area. Consider the three types of bifold doors discussed below.

Manufactured bifold door sets

For large cabinets or armoires, or for built-in storage cabinets, consider using regular bifold doors. These are sold in sets complete with the necessary mounting hardware. Height of these doors is the standard 6 feet 8 inches, and widths range from 2 feet (two 12-inch bifold panels) to 3 feet (two 18-inch bifold panels). By installing two 3-foot sets side by side, you effectively enclose an opening 6 feet wide. Larger spaces can be enclosed by installing more vertical supports and more bifold sets, or by installing special folding door sets in which multiple, accordion-fold panels are suspended from an overhead track.

Projects where a bifold door is particularly useful include an ironing-board cabinet, a case containing a fold-out bed, or a large built-in entertainment center. Any one of these projects may require doors the full 6-foot, 8-inch height. Although bifold doors can be cut down somewhat to fit smaller projects, because of the construction, they cannot be cut down more than 1 or 2 inches in any direction.

Louvered shutters

Appropriate for smaller openings, louvered shutters are attractive and do not require special hardware for installation. Being smaller and lighter, they are especially suitable for bifold installations. The shutters are available with movable slats, but the fixed-slat version is recommended for cabinet doors.

Many precut sizes are available. Buy ones that are as close as possible to the required size and make minor adjustments to fit the opening. Attach panels with high-quality butt hinges; problems with sticking and sagging are directly related to the quality of the hinges used. Remember that, in a bifold installation, 2 of the hinges will have pivots facing outward; on the other 2 hinges, pivots will face inward. Two-way hinges may add to the convenience of reaching the storage area but should be used only with lightweight panels.

Custom bifold doors

An experienced woodworker knows that it is not necessary to buy manufactured bifold door sets or louvered shutters in order to hang bifold doors. In fact, almost all cabinet doors can be mounted in a bifold fashion as long as they are made in a paired set. This is true of inset, flush, lipped, raised-panel, or glazed-panel doors.

As is the case with louvered doors, it is advisable to use high-quality hinges and to keep the weight of the door panels to a minimum. To make sure inset door panels are neatly positioned while being opened and closed, rout a small groove on the bottom of the face-frame member above the opening. Drill a hole in the top corner of the inner bifold panel, and insert a small spring and a loose pin or dowel. This pin tracks in the groove in the face frame. The spring allows you to engage and disengage the pin, as necessary, during installation. Use a magnetic catch as a stop to hold the center of each pair of doors in the closed position, and locate the pull as close to the magnetic catch as possible.

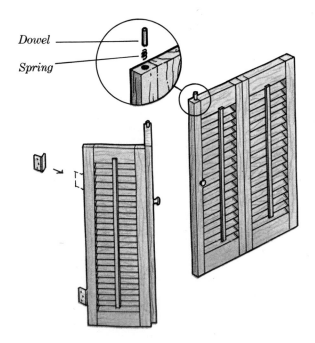

Dowel

Spring

Sliding doors

Using sliding doors is another way to eliminate the swing-out area required by hinged doors. They are also fairly economical and fast to build. Make the panels from plywood, hardboard, plastic, or glass. Unless you have built a pocket opening into which to slide a single panel, the panels must be installed in pairs. Additional panels can be added to the left or right of the main pair, as long as they ride in the same tracks.

Manufactured track

Buy metal or plastic tracks, cut them to length, and install them at the top and bottom of the door opening. Attach the shallower track at the bottom. Cut the sliding panels so that the combined width is 1 inch wider than the opening in the case. The height should correspond to the height of the opening minus an allowance for the lower track. The width of the track channels determines the thickness of the door panels. Most channels are designed to accommodate panels ¼-inch thick.

Track and grooves

Be aware that the track will be visible, unless hidden by a face frame. If this is undesirable, rout grooves in the case in which to install the track. (Remember that you will have to adjust the height and width of the door panels accordingly.)

Routed grooves

For installations where appearance is not a major factor—cabinets in the garage or workshop, for example—the manufactured tracks can be altogether eliminated. Simply rout or cut the grooves directly into the case. Make the grooves ¹/₁₆-inch wider than the door panels. Also, the upper grooves should be twice as deep as the lower ones.

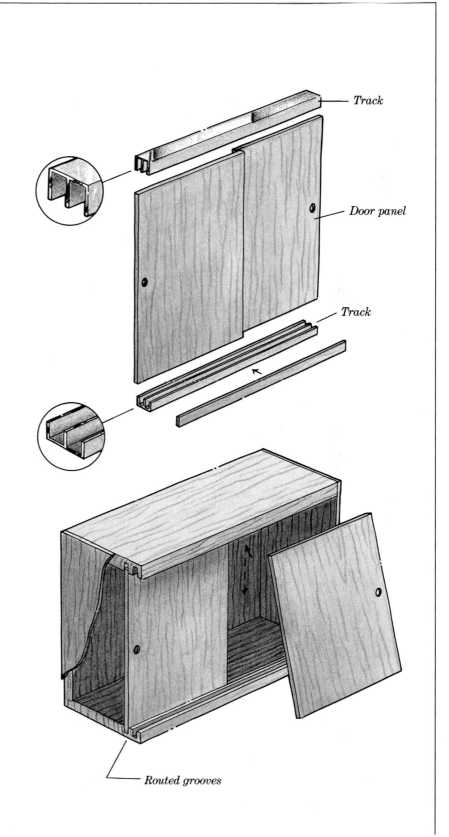

Track

Door panel

Track

Routed grooves

Tongue-and-groove doors

Most often used to create a country or cottage look, tongue-and-groove cabinet doors can be constructed in several ways. Premilled tongue-and-groove boards are manufactured for siding. Thinner premilled pieces intended for use as interior wall panelling are also available.

Using glue and finishing nails, mount the boards directly on pairs of back rails, letting the ends extend beyond the finished dimensions. When glue is dry, trim door panel to the proper size. If you use exterior siding, the panels will be thick enough to be lipped (see Lipped Doors on page 44). Thinner tongue-and-groove boards require heftier back rails, resulting in a door that is suitable for surface-mounting only.

It is possible to create your own tongue-and-groove boards if you have the time and a good router table or shaper. Whether or not you make your own boards, consider different options for your cabinet doors, such as mounting the boards horizontally or at an angle.

These cabinets are carefully crafted so that the flush doors in the buffet align with the glazed panel doors in the wall-mounted unit.

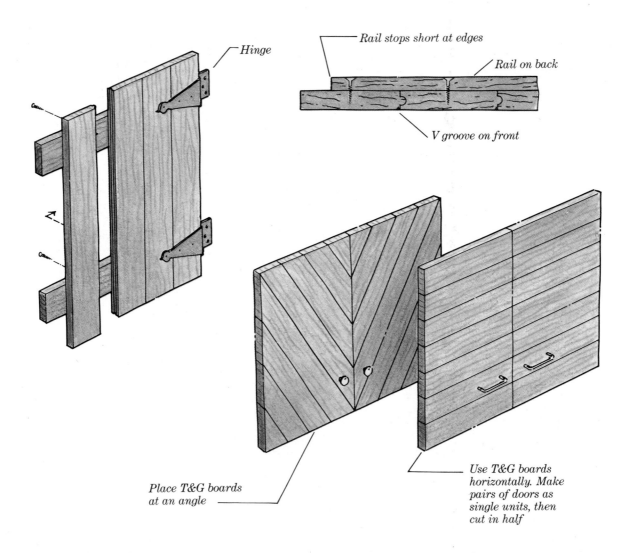

Hinge

Rail stops short at edges

Rail on back

V groove on front

Place T&G boards at an angle

Use T&G boards horizontally. Make pairs of doors as single units, then cut in half

Note: Make mock T&G boards by routing grooves into plywood doors

DRAWERS

Typically installed at waist level or below, drawers provide storage space and relatively convenient access without the stooping that is required by door-fronted cabinets at the same level.

Drawers are not installed at higher levels because it becomes impossible to see what is stored inside. However, slide-out shelves, using inverted drawer construction and the same hardware, can be very useful.

Drawer guides

Drawer guides perform two distinct functions. They serve to locate the drawer as it is opened and closed, much as rails hold a train on track. And the guides also keep the back of the drawer from rising up as the drawer is opened beyond the halfway point. Good guides enable you to open and close a drawer with a smooth, effortless action—even when the drawer is heavily loaded.

Although it is possible to design and build drawer guide systems out of wood, the use of manufactured systems is recommended. These systems are inexpensive, they ensure smooth operation, and maybe best of all, they are adjustable. Two basic types are available, although there are many variations on each type. Check to see what is available in your area, and choose guides before starting drawer construction so that you can take the particular requirements into account.

Side-mounted guides

Although these are generally considered to provide the smoothest operation, side-mounted roller guides necessitate building special side rails. The cabinet case, specifically the area into which the drawer will slide, must have side rails installed from front to back on each side of the opening. These rails can be simple 1 by 2s, but they must be perpendicular to the face frame and must be mounted absolutely parellel to each other. The outer parts of the guides are mounted onto these rails. The inner parts of the guides attach to the sides of the drawer. There is room for some adjustment, but not very much. Two versions of the side-mounted guides are available. One includes a pair of nylon wheels inside each set of tracks; the other has telescoping tracks that ride on ball bearings.

Center-mounted guides

This type of guide does not require additional side rails within the case, as side mounts do, and the cost is generally less. The action, however, is not quite as smooth, especially after extended use. Still, center-mounted guides are quite adequate for drawers in most cabinets.

The normal installation involves nailing or screwing an extendable guide rail to the back of the face frame and to the rear of the cabinet, at the bottom of the opening. A follower is attached to the lower back of the drawer. This follower keeps the drawer centered when it is opened and closed, and prevents the drawer from tipping when it is open. Most of the weight of the drawer is carried on L-shaped guide pads fastened to the lower inside corners of the opening in the face frame. In one version of the center-mounted guide system, L-shaped pads are replaced with rollers. This type, which also has a roller at the back of the drawer, operates more smoothly.

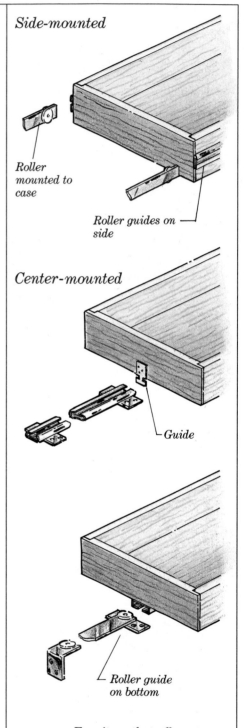

Side-mounted

Roller mounted to case

Roller guides on side

Center-mounted

Guide

Roller guide on bottom

Furniture that offers storage potential allows a room to be put to several uses. In a study/guest bedroom, drawers with channel pulls are file cabinets and the headboard unit doubles as a blanket chest.

Drawer construction

Commercially made drawers often utilize a type of routed dovetail construction. This method of construction is rather involved and requires a router, special bits, and a dovetailing jig. Although this joint is not beyond the scope of the do-it-yourselfer, it is better suited to the production of quantities of drawers where the cost of the equipment and the set-up time required can be amortized over a number of drawers. Unless you are crafting antique reproductions by hand or making a lot of drawers (or boxes), you will find the rabbet-dado-groove method described below satisfactory for most projects. However, to make even the simplest drawers, you will need a table saw or a radial arm saw and a dado blade.

Drawer fronts

Start with the front panel of the drawer, which is composed of either one or two pieces. One-piece construction is sometimes used in the construction of lipped drawer fronts, but the two-piece construction discussed here is adaptable to virtually any drawer. It results in a stronger drawer and one that can be adjusted slightly for fit during construction.

If your cabinet will have both drawers and doors, they should match in style. In fact, you would do well to take measurements from the cabinet case and make all the doors and drawer fronts at the same time. (See the Doors section starting on page 42.)

A note of caution: If you are making drawers to match raised-panel doors, keep in mind that it will be necessary to fasten the front drawer panel to the drawer box. It is recommended that you modify your overall plan so that the drawer fronts are solid panels, perhaps shaped at the edges in a pattern that matches the cabinet doors. This will make them much easier to attach to the box.

When drawer fronts are completed, check them for fit in the face frame of the cabinet. If they are correct, set them aside. You can, if you wish, apply the finish before setting them aside.

Drawer boxes

The next step is to build the drawer boxes onto which the fronts will later be fastened.

Before starting construction, you must have decided these three things about the drawers in your case.
☐ The dimensions of the opening in the face frame
☐ The space requirements of the glides to be used, and
☐ The maximum depth of the drawer box. This may be affected by the type of glide system used. Center-mounted glide systems allow you to build slightly wider drawers than those supported on side-mounted rail systems. They are also a bit more forgiving when it comes to a neat fit.

When making drawers that will be supported on center guides, cut the drawer box 3/8 inch to 1/2 inch narrower than the face-frame opening. This will allow for 3/16 inch to 1/4 inch of space on each side of the drawer.

The gap will, of course, be covered by the front panel when the drawer is closed. Follow the same guidelines when measuring the height of the drawer boxes.

Manufacturer's instructions regarding clearances are generally included with the side-rail hardware. Be sure to read all instructions before you build the boxes.

After determining the dimensions for the drawer boxes, you are ready to lay out the stock and cut pieces to the required lengths.

Look at the illustration below. Note that the pieces fit together in an interlocking pattern, calling for a number of dadoes, rabbets, and grooves. When building several drawer boxes for a particular project, you can save a great deal of time by doing all the layout first, then the cutting, then the dadoes, rabbets, and grooves.

Determine the height of the drawer boxes and, using 1/2-inch plywood, cut the strips that will form the fronts, sides, and backs of the boxes. Cut all the pieces the same height at this time; the rear panels will be cut down later. From these strips, cut pairs of

Drawer fronts

Surface

Lipped

Flush

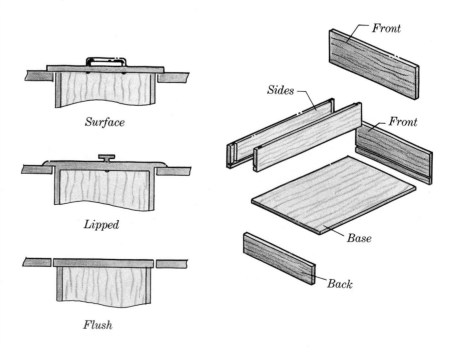

Front

Sides

Front

Base

Back

side panels and matching front and back panels.

Set aside the back panel and, using a dado blade, cut grooves for the drawer base. For example: If the drawer bases will be made from ¼-inch plywood (suitable for most drawers), cut ¼-inch by ¼-inch grooves ½ inch up from the bottom edges of the front panel and both side pieces.

Next, set up the saw to cut the crosswise dadoes and rabbets in the side panels. Dadoes for attaching the back panel should be cut ½ inch from the back of each side panel. Cut rabbets at the front edges that are ½ inch wide and ¼ inch deep.

Measure from the tops of the side panels to the tops of the grooves, and cut back panels to this height. Cut drawer bases out of ¼-inch plywood.

Using glue and ⅝-inch brads, assemble the drawer box pieces in the following order.
□ Attach each of the side panels to the front panel.
□ Slide drawer base into position.
□ Slide back panel down to base.

Place drawer box assembly on a flat surface and check for square. If the box is not square, check that all pieces are seated into the grooves. Nail and glue. When glue is dry, sand boxes and apply finish.

If there will be several drawers stacked one above the other, it is important that the edges of the face frame line up. To do this, wait until the finish is dry then draw an *X* on the front of each drawer box from corner to corner to locate the center. Mount the hardware on the drawers and the cabinet, then slide drawers into the closed position. Using a level and the *X* marked on the front of each drawer box, mark the center point of the drawer box on the face frame as well as on the top and bottom edges. Pull drawer open slightly and extend marks around to the sides of drawer box.

Hold the front panels (which were completed earlier and set aside) up to the face frame and transfer center point marks on all 4 sides to the edges of each drawer front. Remove drawer boxes from cabinet. Position and attach front panels to fronts of the drawer boxes carefully matching the marks you have made.

Drawer pulls

Most hardware and home-center stores offer a large selection of pulls, knobs, and handles that can be mounted on a drawer front—shop around to find the type that appeals. If there are doors as well as drawers in your case, use the same pulls or knobs on both.

Mount the pulls according to the manufacturer's directions. Attaching the pulls usually requires drilling one or more holes into the front of the drawer face. Therefore, choose carefully. If you change your mind at some later date, you will probably have to fill these holes and refinish the drawer front.

For a contemporary, streamlined look, channel track may be more suitable than knobs or pulls. This track is mounted to the top edge and provides a finger slot to enable you to pull the drawer open. If this is your choice, make a flush-mounted drawer and remember to allow for the depth of the channel when you plan the drawer openings in the case.

Drawer construction

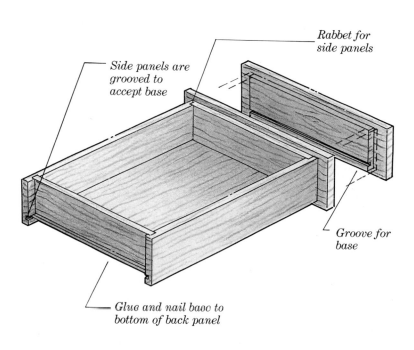

Side panels are grooved to accept base

Rabbet for side panels

Groove for base

Glue and nail base to bottom of back panel

Drawer pulls

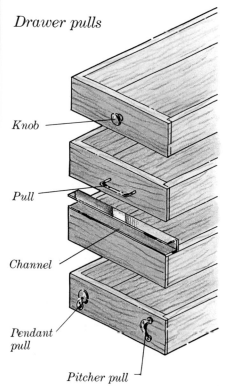

Knob

Pull

Channel

Pendant pull

Pitcher pull

Drawer dividers

The contents of large drawers can be organized with adjustable dividers.

Cut strips of ¼-inch plywood as wide (minus a half inch or so) as the drawer is high. Then cut the strips into appropriate lengths. Cut at least 2 pieces that are as long as the drawer is deep (measure from inside front to inside back) and 2 or more that are as long as the drawer is wide (inside dimensions again).

Stack pieces together and cut a series of ¼-inch-wide slots into them. Use a dado blade to cut these slots so that they extend just beyond the mid-point of the width of the boards. Space the slots every 2 inches or at points where dividers are desired. After sanding and painting, dividers are ready to slide together and drop into the most cluttered drawers.

Slide-outs

A variation on standard drawer construction, these traylike drawers are good for stowing bulky items in low cabinets—items such as small appliances, pots and pans, canned goods, a slide projector, and file boxes.

Make the base of the tray from a sturdy piece of ¾-inch plywood and the sides from 1 by 3 pine. Be sure that drawers are narrow enough so that they will slide out when cabinet doors are open. Add 1 by 2 rails to the inside of the cabinet if necessary.

Using a dado blade, cut ⅜-inch by ¾-inch rabbets along bottom edge and back end of each side panel and at both ends of the front panel (see details on illustration).

Assemble sides and bottom using 4-penny (4d) finishing nails and a liberal amount of glue. When glue is dry, sand, paint, and install side-mounted roller guides, as described on page 50.

Drawer dividers

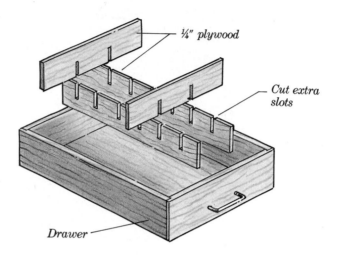

¼" plywood

Cut extra slots

Drawer

Slide-outs

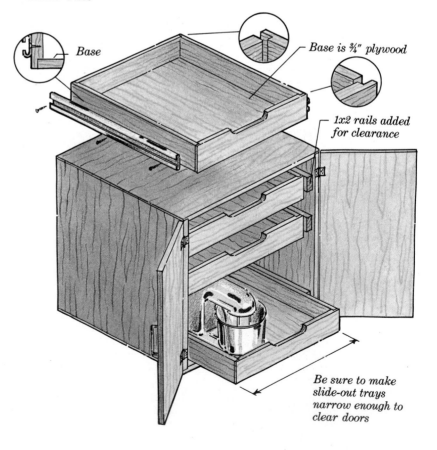

Base

Base is ¾" plywood

1x2 rails added for clearance

Be sure to make slide-out trays narrow enough to clear doors

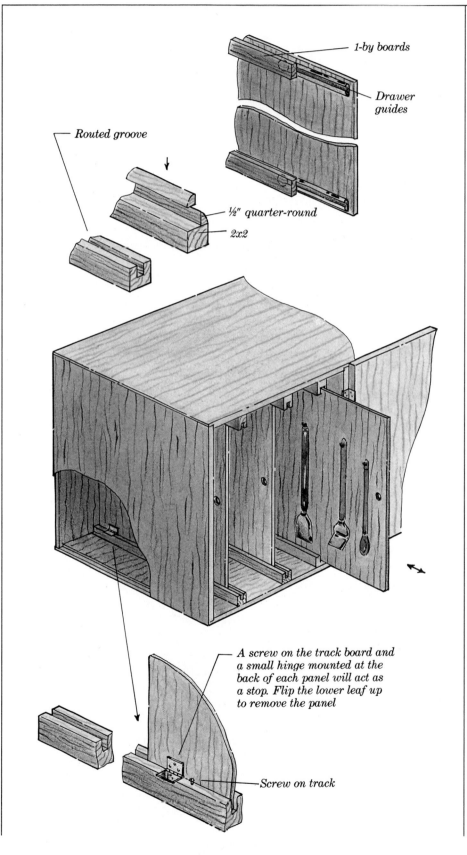

1-by boards

Drawer guides

Routed groove

½" quarter-round

2x2

A screw on the track board and a small hinge mounted at the back of each panel will act as a stop. Flip the lower leaf up to remove the panel

Screw on track

Vertical drawers

Vertical drawers are not drawers at all but, rather, vertical sliding panels. Make the sliding version for hanging long or flat utensils that cause a jumble when stored in a drawer. The same construction methods can also be used to create vertical storage space for items such as baking sheets and serving platters. The fact that the dividers will slide out is an advantage when you want to clean the cabinet.

The dividers do not extend the full depth; however, the tracks in which they slide do (see illustration). This gives extra support when dividers are pulled out and allows shelves to be hung on the inside of cabinet doors.

Make panels from ¼-inch plywood or perforated hardboard. If you plan to hang heavy items on the panels, such as iron trivets or a griddle, use ⅜-inch plywood instead.

Make tracks by gluing and nailing lengths of quarter-round to a 2 by 2, or by routing a groove directly into a solid board. For easier operation, mount drawer glides (either the roller or telescoping type) to the panels. Install 1-by boards on edge inside the cabinet and fasten the stationary part of the glide hardware onto these boards. The shape of the inside of your cabinet and the way in which the doors are hung will determine the exact size of the boards needed.

When planning vertical drawers, remember to leave enough space between panels to allow storage on both sides of each panel. As shown in the illustration, a screw driven into the bottom track board and a small hinge placed at the lower back of the panel act as a stop. Lift lower leaf of hinge to bypass screw when you need to remove the panel.

COMPUTER CENTER

T his add-on unit is specially planned to accommodate a personal computer. In the illustration, you can see that it has been designed to fit into an existing bookcase, which originally was not deep enough and had no special provisions for the computer.

Among the features included in the design is a shelf for a keyboard, at typing height; shelves that can be adjusted to suit a variety of computers; and holes and slots for cables, cords, and printer paper stored in the cabinet below.

This project can also be built as a freestanding unit simply by extending side panels down to the floor and adding a back. The design can be adapted to a general-purpose writing desk by installing the unit higher (29 inches is standard desk height) and eliminating the holes and slots.

Dimensions

Many personal computers fit onto shelves 16 inches deep but a few larger models require a shelf 19 inches deep. Measure your computer when you plan the case, being certain to include the depth of the cable connectors (generally located at the back) in your measurements.

The bottom of the case should be at typing height, typically 26 to 27 inches above the floor. As the case is 34 inches high, this puts the top approximately 60 inches above the floor, a convenient height for storing tall or flat items.

If the case will be inserted into an existing bookcase, use inside dimensions to determine the width of this project. On the other hand, if you are building a freestanding unit, make it

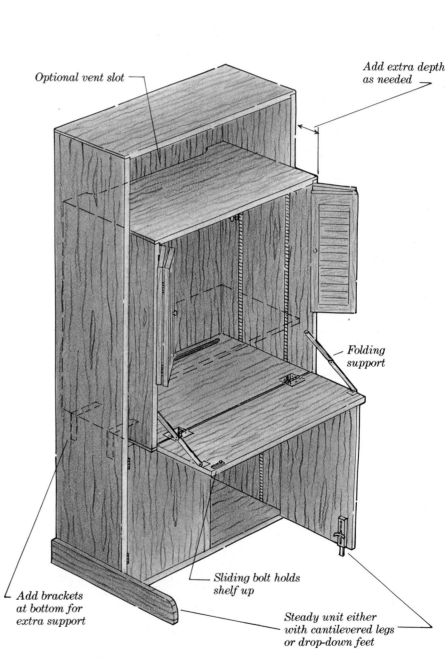

Optional vent slot

Add extra depth as needed

Folding support

Add brackets at bottom for extra support

Sliding bolt holds shelf up

Steady unit either with cantilevered legs or drop-down feet

Note: A slot at back of desk allows you to feed paper to a printer. Drill holes for cords and cables

any width appropriate for your computer. Bear in mind that shelves or surfaces wider than 30 inches either need vertical dividers or stronger shelving (see page 36).

Building the case

Once you have determined dimensions for your case, building it is a straightforward process. Cut top and bottom panels out of hardwood-veneered lumber-core plywood. From the same material, cut side panels to height of cavity. Drill and cut required holes and slots in the bottom panel. Rout dadoes for shelf standards and rabbets for back panel, if you are attaching one.

Fit pieces together, gluing and nailing top to sides and gluing and screwing bottom to sides; use 2-inch screws every 4 inches. Secure back, if there is one, with glue and brads.

Calculate the area of surfaces that will overhang your case when desk unit is mounted. Apply veneer to all visible surfaces. After trimming the sides, glue veneer onto front edges of case. This covers with hardwood all exposed edges except the holes and slots in the bottom. These can be painted black later.

Building the desk

Cut a piece of plywood for the flip-down typing surface. Measure this piece so that it fits inside the front opening of case. Be sure to allow for thickness of veneer that will face the edges. A 10-inch-deep shelf will hold most computer keyboards. Taking measurements from folding supports you plan to use, mark and cut rabbets in edges of shelf to accommodate brackets when shelf is in up position.

After applying veneer to the edges of shelf, check it for fit, then hinge shelf onto bottom front of the case. Cut accurate mortises into shelf and case to accept hinge leaves.

Finishing the case

Select doors and trim them to fit upper portion of case. (The illustration shows bifold doors but you can select other types. See Doors starting on page 42.) Mount doors to check them for fit, then remove doors and shelf from case and finish all pieces.

When the finish is dry, mount computer desk into your bookcase, using 6 or 8 screws per side. For extra support, attach two 2-inch L brackets at the bottom of sides of the bookcase. Mount flip-down shelf, sliding bolt or magnetic catches, shelf standards, and doors.

Before setting the computer in place, either secure the whole bookcase to the wall by screwing it to studs, or add stabilizer feet at the bottom (see illustration) to keep the cabinet from tipping forward. Sturdy doors at the bottom of the unit can also serve as stabilizers.

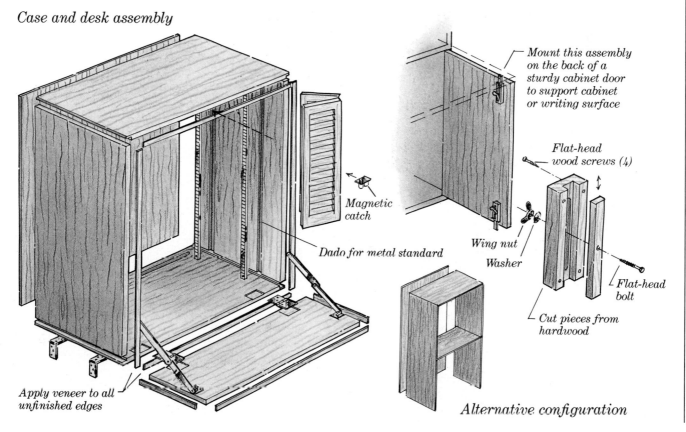

Case and desk assembly

Magnetic catch

Dado for metal standard

Apply veneer to all unfinished edges

Mount this assembly on the back of a sturdy cabinet door to support cabinet or writing surface

Flat-head wood screws (4)

Wing nut

Washer

Flat-head bolt

Cut pieces from hardwood

Alternative configuration

HIDDEN DOUBLE-BED CABINET

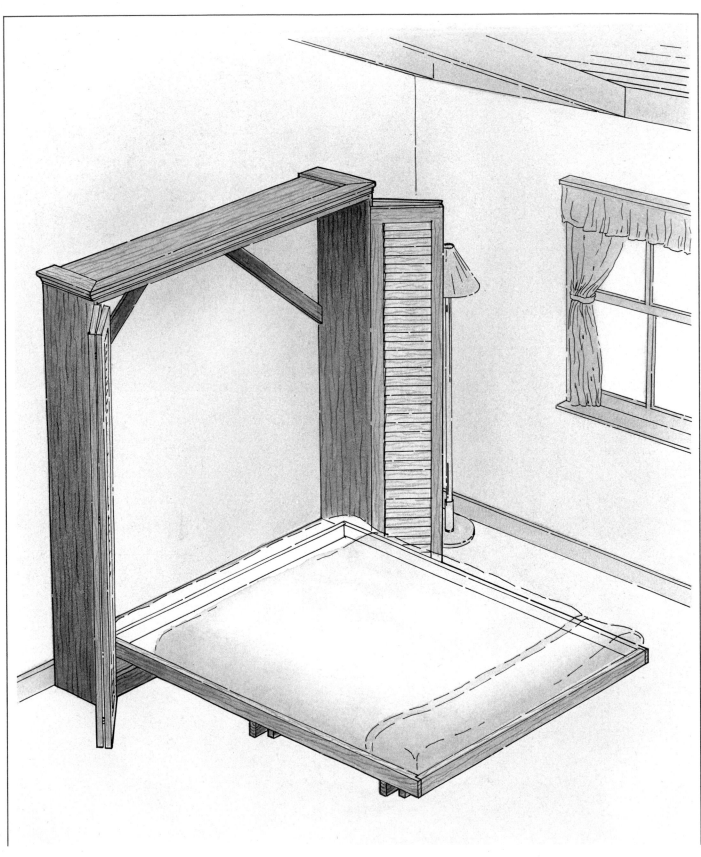

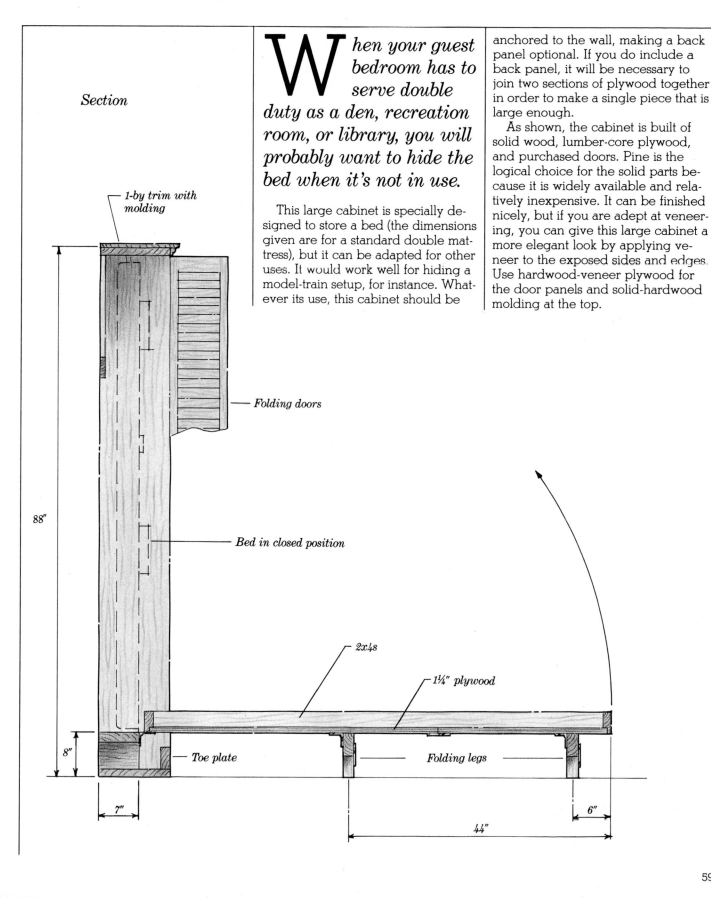

Section

1-by trim with molding

Folding doors

88"

Bed in closed position

2x4s

1¼" plywood

8"

Toe plate

Folding legs

7"

6"

44"

W hen your guest bedroom has to serve double duty as a den, recreation room, or library, you will probably want to hide the bed when it's not in use.

This large cabinet is specially designed to store a bed (the dimensions given are for a standard double mattress), but it can be adapted for other uses. It would work well for hiding a model-train setup, for instance. Whatever its use, this cabinet should be anchored to the wall, making a back panel optional. If you do include a back panel, it will be necessary to join two sections of plywood together in order to make a single piece that is large enough.

As shown, the cabinet is built of solid wood, lumber-core plywood, and purchased doors. Pine is the logical choice for the solid parts because it is widely available and relatively inexpensive. It can be finished nicely, but if you are adept at veneering, you can give this large cabinet a more elegant look by applying veneer to the exposed sides and edges. Use hardwood-veneer plywood for the door panels and solid-hardwood molding at the top.

Cabinet construction

- Sides
- Ends
- 88"
- 64½"
- 2x12s

Cabinet box

Using select 2 by 12 pine, cut sides 88 inches long and top and bottom pieces 64½ inches long. These dimensions allow a 3-inch clearance on each side of mattress-box assembly. The 3-inch spaces are necessary so that mattress box clears doors when they are in the folded-back position. Determine exactly how much space will be required by the doors and hinges you select and build the case accordingly. Even if doors fold completely out of the way, allow 1 inch on each side, to be safe. Cut rabbets at ends of side pieces and, if installing a back panel, along back edges. Glue and nail main case together.

Build a support shelf into bottom of main case using 2-by material 63 inches long, ripped to 7 inches wide. Attach top of support shelf 8 inches above outside bottom of case. Add 3

bolsters (see illustration) also cut from 2-by material.

Trim top of case with 3 glued-on pieces of mitered 1-by material. Overhang pieces 1 inch at sides and front, and skirt pieces with molding, mitered at the corners.

Lowering mechanism

Manufactured fold-up beds in cabinets utilize a spring mechanism to facilitate raising and lowering the mattress platform. These mechanisms can be purchased with or without the bed base.

In this version, the bed can be raised and lowered with a pulley, making it easier to both pull the bed down and push it back up. If you use the pulley system, install let-in braces at top of case. Make braces from 1 by 3 or 1 by 4 material.

Finish the case and set it into position. Use L brackets to secure case to wall, driving screws into studs.

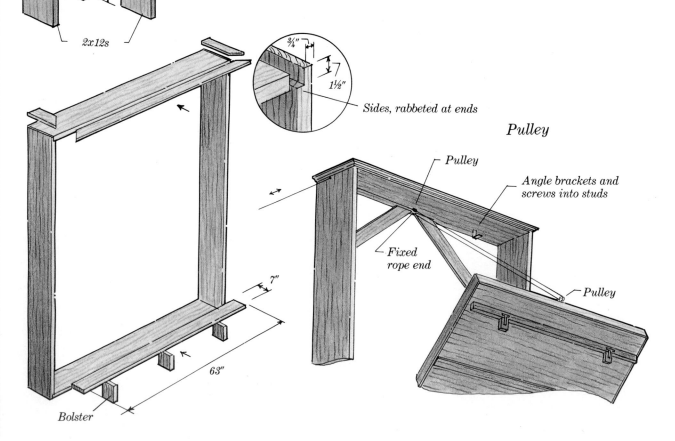

¾"

1½"

Sides, rabbeted at ends

Pulley

Pulley

Angle brackets and screws into studs

Fixed rope end

Pulley

7"

63"

Bolster

Mattress box

The mattress box consists of a 55½ by 76½ inch platform of ¾-inch lumber-core plywood (2 pieces joined with a 55½ inch length of 1 by 4) nested into a frame of select-grade 2 by 4s.

Cut side pieces 78 inches long and end pieces 55½ inches long. Rabbet ends of side pieces as well as bottom inside edge of all 4 pieces. Screw and glue rails together, and nail and glue bottom platform in place.

Using select-grade 2 by 4s, make folding-leg assemblies to dimensions shown on the illustration. Hinge these assemblies to bottom of mattress platform. Place 1 folding leg 6 inches from the foot of the bed; the other, 44 inches. Apply finish to assembly, let it dry, then hinge box to case using three 3-inch hinges.

Finishing the cabinet

Louvered shutter doors are a good choice on a bed cabinet because they allow air circulation when cabinet is closed; use the bifold type. If doors are a bit short (80-inch-long ones will be), set in a toe plate across bottom of case.

Install a sliding bolt to keep mattress in the stowed position.

Attach four 1-inch-wide nylon webbing straps. Screw webbing to inside of mattress box rails using 2 oval-head screws and finish washers per strap. These straps hold mattress and bedding in place when bed is in the stowed position. Attach patches of Velcro® or sew D rings to strap ends.

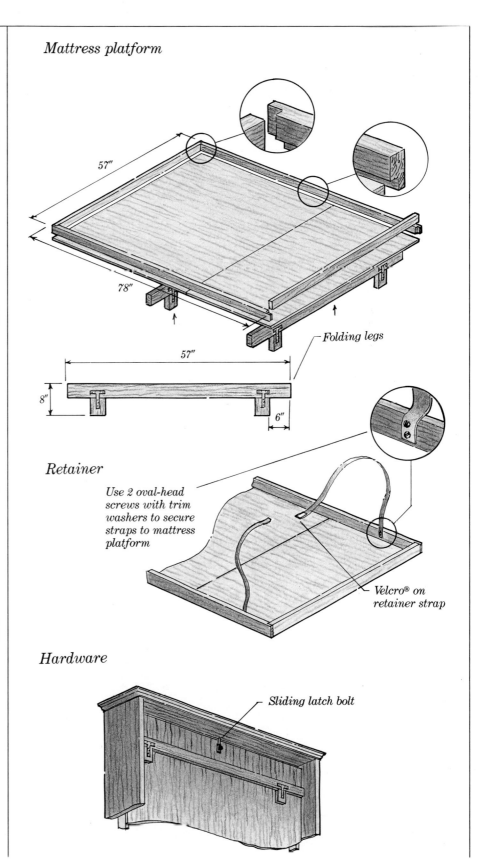

Mattress platform

57"

78"

57"

8"

6"

Folding legs

Retainer

Use 2 oval-head screws with trim washers to secure straps to mattress platform

Velcro® on retainer strap

Hardware

Sliding latch bolt

SLIDE-PROJECTOR CABINET

I*f your great slide col-lection remains un-seen because of the trouble involved in setting up the projector, consider building this projector cabinet. Guests might even appreciate your collection more if they frequently see a few slides at a time, rather than a large quan-tity all at once.*

This project involves outfitting a basic corner cabinet to accommodate a circular-tray projector, a roll-up screen, and trays of slides.

In this triangular cabinet two of the sides are 27½ inches wide; the third (the front) is 39 inches. This results in a rather wide cabinet with shelves deep enough to hold a projector. However, the outer corners are chamfered (beveled), and because the cabinet is in a corner, it does not appear too large. The 72-inch height provides ample storage space and allows the projector to be placed high enough to miss the heads of seated viewers.

The basic corner cabinet, as shown, can be built from 2 sheets of plywood and 2 by 4s and 1 by 2s. To outfit the cabinet for the projector, you will need an additional sheet of plywood for the shelves and 1 by 2s to support them. Metal standards and shelf clips allow shelves to be ad-justed and eliminate need for cleats.

As seen in the illustration, shelves are cut away to make a niche for storing the roll-up screen. By allow-ing 12 inches between shelves, each can store 6 tray boxes on end. Drill a 1¼-inch hole in an unobtrusive place through which to thread power cord.

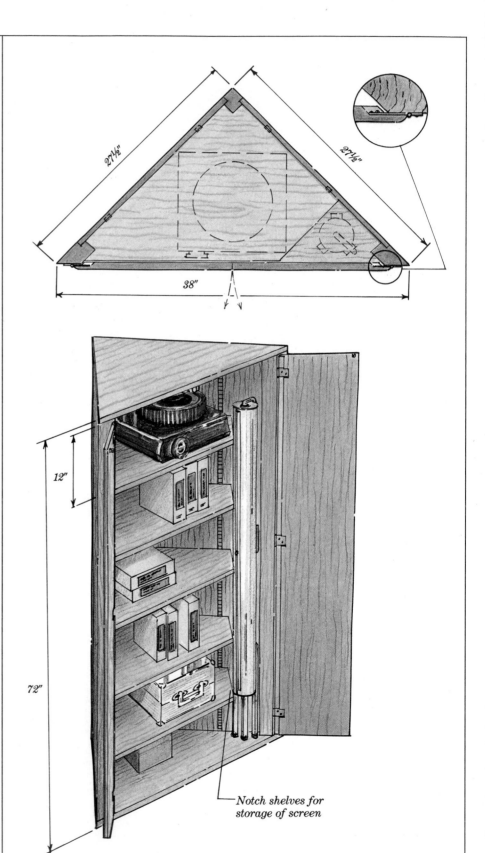

27½"   27½"

38"

12"

72"

Notch shelves for
storage of screen

WINE RACK

This easy-to-build wine rack can be used as a freestanding unit, or it can be built into an existing cabinet.

Increase or decrease height and width to fit your needs or the space available for the rack. To do so, lengthen front and back crosspieces in 3¼-inch increments, and the height of the side panels in 3½-inch increments.

Building the rack

Make side panels from a length of 1 by 12 or 2 by 12 stock, the crosspieces from 1 by 2 stock, and bottle supports from 1¼-inch-diameter closet pole.

Drill side panels with starter holes for cut-out handles and leg recesses. Cut panels, crosspieces, and round bottle supports to length. Sand and finish all pieces.

Carefully mark and drill pilot holes in crosspieces and bottle supports. Using 2-inch by No.8 round-head brass wood screws, join these parts to form ladderlike subassemblies. Mark and drill side panels, then screw assembled ladder shelves to them using two 1½-inch by No.6 round-head brass wood screws. Your wine rack is ready to use: *à votre santé.*

Variations

The materials and assembly techniques for this basic wine rack may be modified in several ways.
☐ Substitute flat-head screws for round-head screws, but remember to countersink them or to counterbore screw holes and cover heads with wooden plugs.
☐ Eliminate screws altogether and substitute glued dowels.
☐ Use metal or plastic horizontal crosspieces. Screw them to front edges of side panels.

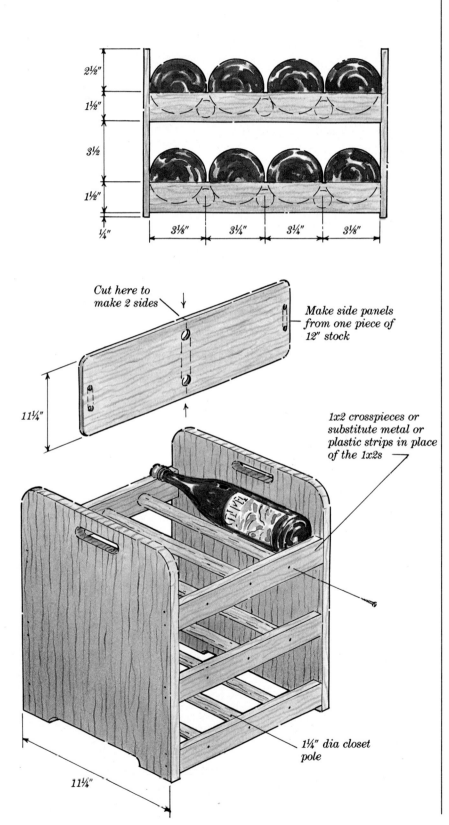

2½"
1½"
3½
1½"
¼"
3⅛" 3¼" 3¼" 3⅛"

Cut here to make 2 sides

Make side panels from one piece of 12" stock

11¼"

1x2 crosspieces or substitute metal or plastic strips in place of the 1x2s

1¼" dia closet pole

11¼"

SEWING CENTER

If you like to sew, but find that sometimes it's just too much trouble to get out the machine, here's the solution. This sewing center, built into a new or existing cabinet, not only puts the machine at your fingertips in a flash, but provides needed work surface as well.

Build this accessory into a sturdy cabinet or, if need be, secure an existing bookcase cabinet to the wall to make the sewing center more stable. Most sewing machines require a shelf 9 to 10 inches deep.

The project described here consists of the sewing shelf only. If you plan to build the complete cabinet, including the sewing shelf, choose a basic case design (see page 80). Integrate the projects as necessary when deciding on dimensions. For instance, if the worktable is to be 36 inches wide, build a basic cabinet with at least one bay that is 36 inches wide and high enough to accommodate the worktable when it is in the closed position.

The fold-down work surface opens to reveal the machine in its stored position. Shelves above the machine hold the accessories and materials used most often. Other supplies can be stored in the drawers and cabinets under and around the work surface.

Before installing the sewing table, determine the most comfortable working height, generally between 26 and 28 inches from the floor. Test the height with the actual machine placed on the trial surface. Make the table wide enough to hold the machine comfortably (usually 18 to 20 inches is sufficient) or as wide as the bay in the bookcase into which it will be installed. If you are building a special case for this project, 36 inches is a good width.

The following instructions describe two versions of a sewing center.

Version one

The flat work surface of this unit can be marked with a grid that is convenient for layout and pattern work. Using this design requires that the machine be lifted from its storage area at the back of the table and placed out of the way.

Version two

This is the same as the first version except for a movable tray to hold the machine. The tray slides along grooves routed into the surface of the shelf and table (the tabletop is not smooth). If the machine is used frequently and put away after each session, the added convenience makes routing grooves and doing necessary extra construction worthwhile.

Rolling tray

Make the tray out of ¾-inch plywood and slightly larger than the base of the machine.

Buy 6 small mounted wheels (see illustration opposite). After drilling 6 holes in the tray, mount wheels from the top. Don't make holes any larger

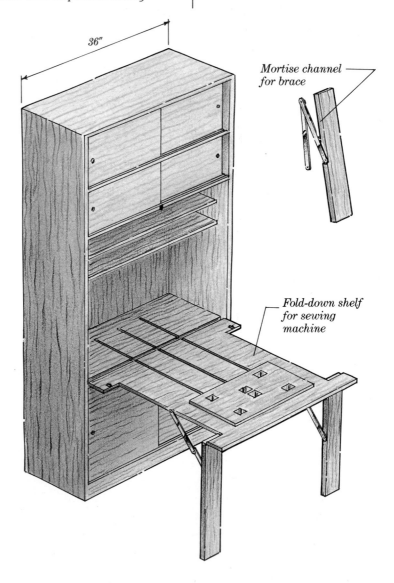

36"

Mortise channel for brace

Fold-down shelf for sewing machine

than necessary. Set the 2 center wheels close together; they support the tray as it is rolled over the gap where the table meets the shelf. To make guides for wheels, rout 3 grooves into top of both table and shelf. Make grooves ⅛-inch deep and as wide as the wheels.

Building the table

Measure the width and height of the bay that will house the sewing table, then subtract ⅛ inch from the width and ¼ inch from the height. Using these dimensions, cut the table from a sheet of ¾-inch solid-core or furniture-grade plywood. Choose a veneered plywood to give the cabinet a finished look when table is in the closed position.

Cut 3½-inch-wide notches to accommodate the legs. Length of notches depends on length of legs; cut accordingly. Using ¾-inch plywood or 1 by 4 stock, make legs to fit the notches.

Using the same ¾-inch plywood stock as for the tabletop, cut a piece to cover the shelf on which the sewing machine will be stored. The plywood will raise the surface of the shelf to the same height as the work surface. It also strengthens the shelf that will support the work surface. Cut the piece of plywood ¾ inch narrower (from front to back) than the shelf, so that the table, when folded up, lies flush with the front face of the case. Lay out and rout the grooves for the rolling machine tray, if installing one.

You will need a 1½-inch piano (continuous) hinge as long as the work surface is wide, or a longer one cut to size with a hacksaw; 2 hinges 1½ inches wide by 3½ inches long to attach legs; and 3 sliding-bolt latches (1 to secure each leg and 1 to hold work surface in closed position).

Assembly

Before assembling the pieces, check for fit, then sand and finish them.

Fasten legs to work table using a pair of 3½-inch-long hinges. Place smaller plywood sheet onto shelf in cabinet, and secure it with several screws placed at the ends and along the front edge. Attach fold-up work surface to cabinet by first screwing piano hinge to back edge of plywood, then to top front edge of shelf.

Attaching the hardware

Position legs vertically (with table flat) and hold an open locking brace at a 45-degree angle as you mark the points on the edges of the table and legs for the locking brace screws. Drill pilot holes and screw braces in place. For a more finished appearance, mark position of locking braces with legs folded up, and rout a mortise channel in the edge of each leg for the brace. You will have to remove legs and braces to do this.

Mount the remaining bolt latches. Place small round-head wood screws in the routed grooves of the tabletop, approximately ½ inch from the ends. The wheels will roll over heads of screws when tray is pulled forward, but they (combined with the weight of the sewing machine) will prevent the tray from rolling backward.

Rolling tray

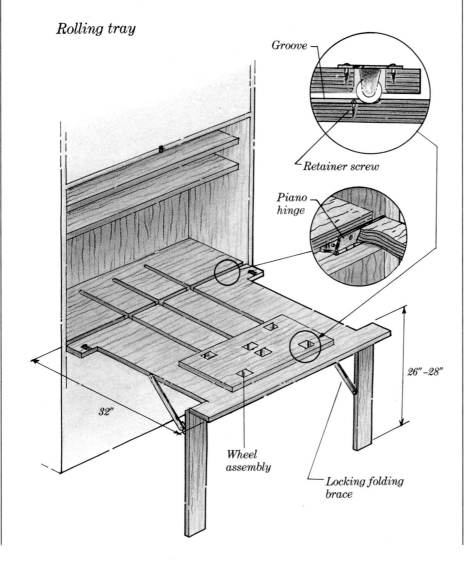

Groove

Retainer screw

Piano hinge

Wheel assembly

Locking folding brace

32"

26"–28"

TV OR STEREO CABINET

Cabinets designed to house electronic entertainment equipment should be as attractive as they are functional. Fine craftsmanship and well-chosen materials will ensure both.

A good design incorporates features that make equipment accessible such as bifold doors (see page 46), a slide-out shelf (see page 54), slotted shelf standards with clips (see page 39), drawers (see page 50), and cabinet doors (see page 42). In addition, here are some other ideas to help you create a special piece of furniture.

Flip-up top

The top of a 3- to 4-foot tall cabinet makes a convenient place to locate a record player. A flip-up top on the cabinet hides the turntable when it is not in use and protects it from dust and accidental damage.

To build this feature into your cabinet, first measure your turntable. Plan an appropriately sized cavity to accommodate your unit. (If you foresee changing your equipment in the near future, allow some extra space.)

Extend the side panels of the cabinet so that they form the sides of the cavity. When working out the height, include the thickness of the shelf and top cover (usually ¾ inch plus ¾ inch). Cut the back panel ¾ inch shorter than the side panels.

Set in top shelf, extending it to the front, so that the lower front edge of the flip-up top rests on it when in the closed position.

Cut flip-up top out of ¾-inch plywood. Make top as deep as side panels of cabinet and add a front lip of the proper height. Reinforce joint between top and front with a triangular wood cleat glued on the inside

of the joint. Hinge top to back panel of cabinet with a continuous hinge fixed along the outside back. Use 1 locking sliding stay to hold top open, or 2 friction-type sliding stays, 1 at each side of the top assembly.

It is recommended that you build this project with hardwood-veneered plywood and use standard finish carpentry techniques to finish all exposed edges and joints.

Double-walled back

To hide the mass of wires that coils and tangles behind electronic equipment, build a double wall to act as the back of the cabinet.

Cut the inner wall from a sturdy material such as ½-inch plywood or particleboard. Drill a pattern of 1¼-inch holes in this sheet, making at least 2 holes for each shelf to be installed in the cabinet. Fix this wall into position 3 inches in front of where the second wall will be attached (see illustration opposite).

Cut a second panel (the outer back wall) from lighter material such as perforated hardboard or ¼-inch plywood. Mount this panel at the back of the cabinet, hinging it at the bottom and securing it at the top with 1 or 2 sliding-bolt latches. You can open this panel to route and arrange the cords and wires leading to the equipment in the cabinet.

The 3-inch space between the walls allows you to install a multiple-outlet strip, so that you can power all the equipment in the cabinet from 1 incoming cord. To avoid causing a hum in the sound system, try to keep power cords separate from signal wires by feeding them through separate holes rather than coiling them around each other.

If you are worried about the equipment overheating, drill some extra 1¼-inch-diameter holes near the top of each panel for convection cooling,

or install a cooling fan at the inside top of the outer panel. Place fan so that it draws cooling air through the holes in the inner back panel. Cooling fans are available at electrical supply stores.

If the cabinet is topped by the flip-up turntable bay described above, extend the double-walled cavity only to the bottom of the shelf that supports the turntable. By drilling 1 or 2 holes at the back of the shelf, you can feed the turntable wiring, between the double walls.

General considerations

When designing and outfitting an entertainment center, you should observe a few conventions and recommended precautions.

☐ Video cassettes, audio cassettes, reels of audiotape, and even computer disks can be ruined by magnetic fields. Therefore, store them away from amplifiers, televisions, and speakers, all of which produce magnetic fields.

☐ Speakers and televisions interact magnetically when placed next to each other. Don't build a cabinet where the speakers are housed next to the TV, unless the TV and the speakers are specially designed for this arrangement.

☐ Keep cassettes and records away from heat. If you store them in the equipment cabinet, place them at the bottom (heat rises) or use a fan to cool the cabinet.

☐ Record collections are heavy. If you plan to store your collection in the cabinet, build an especially sturdy unit.

☐ Television sets come in a variety of sizes, but electronic equipment, including VCR's is rarely wider than 19 inches. This is handy to know when designing your cabinet. Most equipment will fit on shelves 16 inches deep; narrower shelves may be adequate for your equipment.

Top view

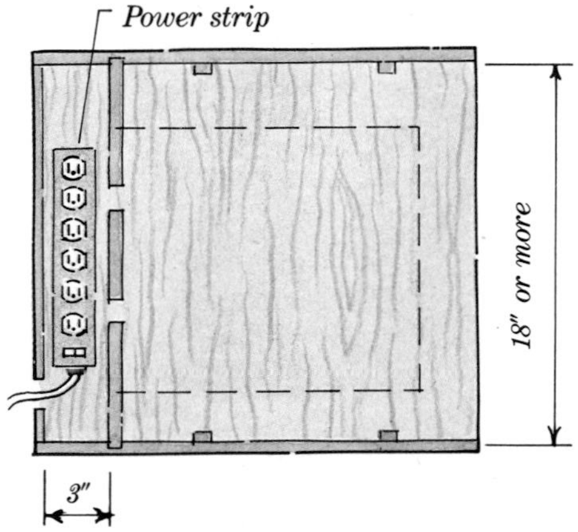

Power strip

18" or more

3"

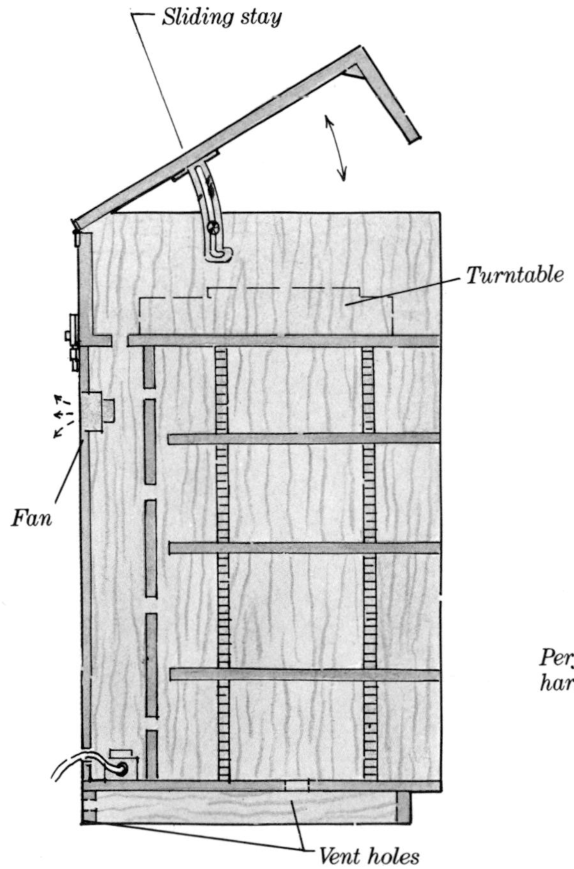

Sliding stay

Turntable

Fan

Vent holes

Side view

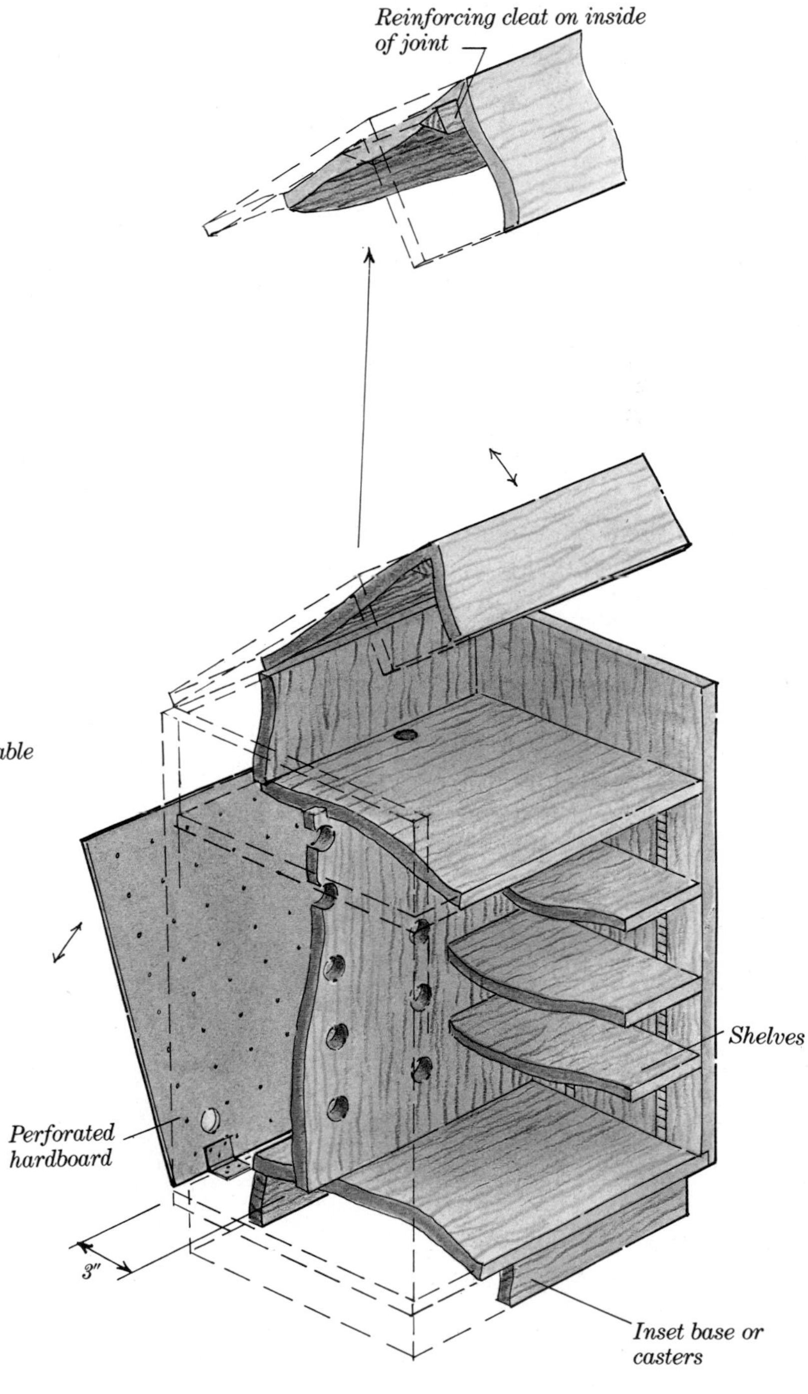

Reinforcing cleat on inside
of joint

Shelves

Perforated
hardboard

3"

Inset base or
casters

IRONING-BOARD CABINET

Insert this fold-away ironing-board unit into a tall cabinet in the laundry room or bedroom. A cabinet made out of ¾-inch plywood, such as the one described on page 80, would be suitable. Readily available materials are used to create this handy and compact project that fits inside.

The outer dimensions of the cabinet shown are 25½ inches by 74 inches by 9¼ inches, large enough to stow the ironing board with space left for a stack of narrow shelves. Here's how to outfit the cabinet for ironing.

Making the board

Start by cutting the ironing board from a sheet of ¾-inch plywood or from a length of 1 by 16 board (although not common, this size is available). Making the ironing board out of 2-by material is even better, but you will have to edge-glue narrower pieces together.

Cut a 15⅞-inch length of closet pole, and attach it to the back of the ironing board with two 6-inch sections of 1 by 2, using 1½-inch by No.8 round-head wood screws.

Attaching the board

Cut two 24-inch lengths of 1 by 8 and, using the end of the closet pole, draw 3 circles on each piece. Connect the circles to form the elongated figure-7 shape shown in the inset illustration. Cut around the marked shape with a saber saw, taking care that the resulting slot is wide enough

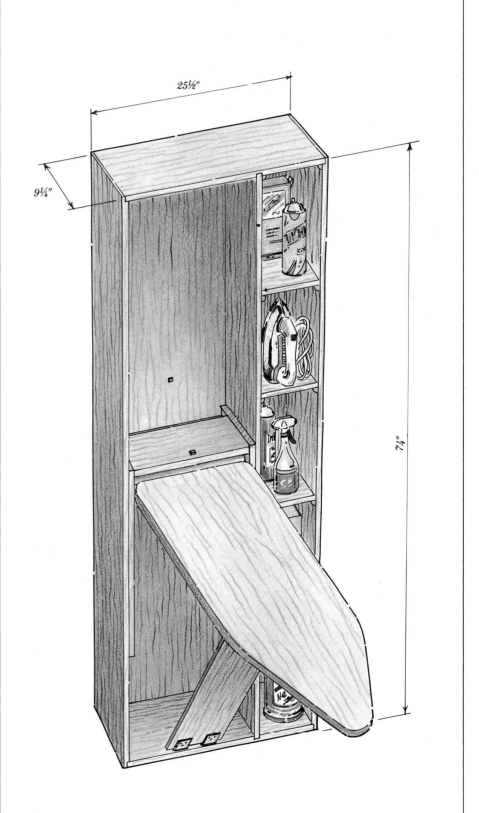

25½"

9¼"

74"

to allow the closet pole to slide without binding.

Screw slotted panels to inside of cabinet. The top of the figure 7 establishes the top of the ironing board; standard height ranges from 32 inches to 35 inches. Use your current ironing board, or a friend's, to determine the height that suits you best.

Cut a length of 1 by 8 to 43 inches. Bevel 1 end about 15 degrees. Attach it to the bottom of the cabinet, in the center with 2 hinges. Using the 1 by 8, cut a small shelf 14 inches wide.

Attach a 1 by 2 cleat across the back of the cabinet so that the top edge is at the same height as the top of the figure 7. Fasten shelf to cleat using 2 small hinges. Holding shelf in the up position, lift ironing-board assembly into position: The back should be supported in the figure-7 slots and the front rests on the floor. Lower shelf onto closet pole, and mark the position for the 2 small wedges on the bottom of shelf. Cut wedges from 1-by material, and attach them securely

to bottom of shelf, just to the outside of the 1 by 2 connectors. These wedges keep closet pole in the forward position when ironing board is in use.

Place a carpenter's level on the ironing board, and holding it level, mark the correct location of brace board on the bottom. Then, using another hinge, attach brace to bottom of the ironing board.

Finally, attach a magnetic latch to the folding shelf and cabinet back. This will hold shelf in the up position.

Cabinet construction

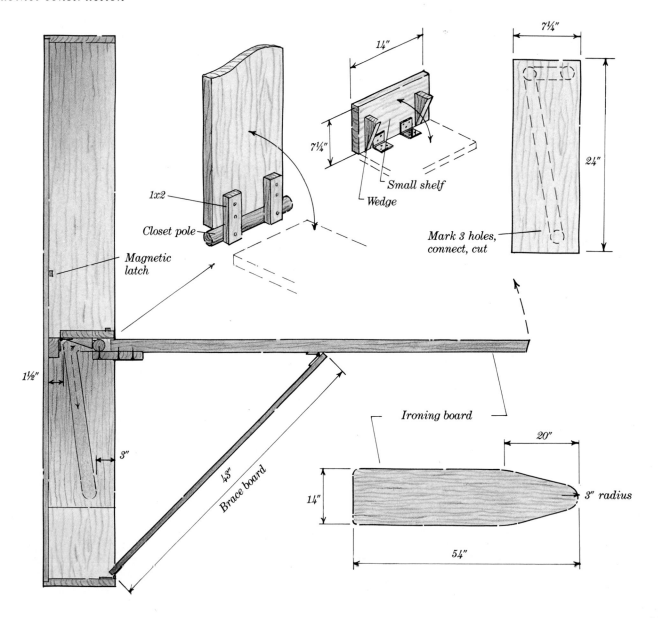

69

BUILDING CASES

T he basic structures presented in this chapter are designed to cover most situations. But if the sizes don't work for you, change them.

There are directions and illustrations for building basic cabinets that can be laminated to serve us kitchen cabinets or veneered and used as bars or buffets. You can build just one tall bookcase to fit between two doors or join several together to fill an alcove. The case can be finished on the back if placed as a room divider or fastened to the wall.

For those looking for instant storage with a minimum of trouble, the first section covers ideas for stacking and finishing manufactured cubes.

Clever selection of materials, fine carpentry, and careful finishing coordinates the variety of bookcases and shelves in this room.

MODULAR CUBES

One ready-made source for a storage wall is cubes made from particleboard or any of the family of related products. The most widely available version is a 5-sided (open on one side) 16-inch cube built out of ⅝-inch particleboard. The joints are rabbeted, and the boxes are machine-sanded.

Assembled cubes are reasonably priced and are generally well finished, considering the material. They are very bulky, however, and may require making several trips to the lumberyard in order to get all that you need. If this is a problem, you can buy knocked-down versions. These kits require assembling the cubes, filling the gaps, and sanding them yourself.

Among the many variations are double-size (32-inch-wide) rectangles with or without dividers, single cubes with compartments, and drawer boxes that slide into the cubes.

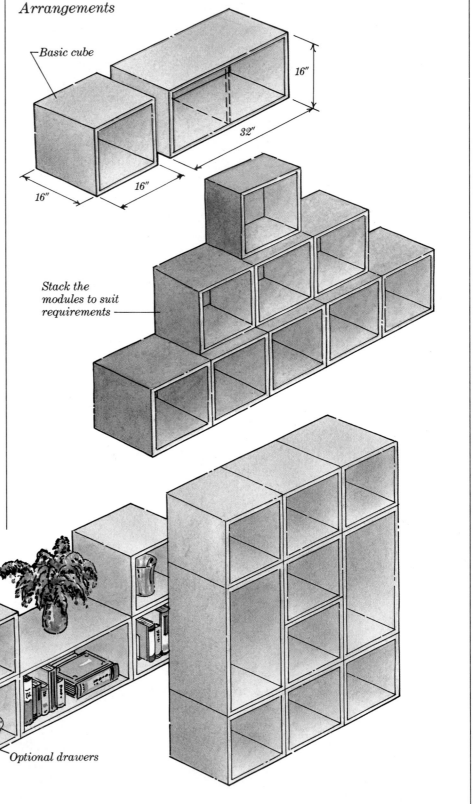

Arrangements

—Basic cube

16"

32"

16"

16"

Stack the modules to suit requirements —

Optional drawers

Modifications

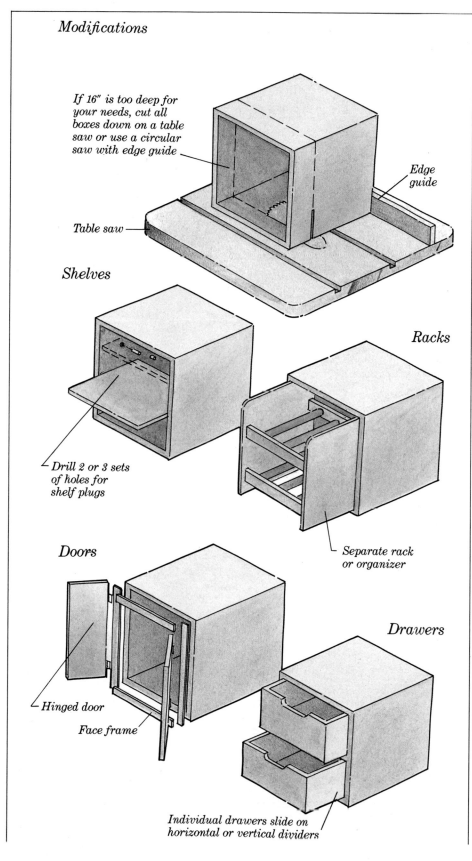

If 16" is too deep for your needs, cut all boxes down on a table saw or use a circular saw with edge guide

Edge guide

Table saw

Shelves

Drill 2 or 3 sets of holes for shelf plugs

Racks

Separate rack or organizer

Doors

Hinged door

Face frame

Drawers

Individual drawers slide on horizontal or vertical dividers

Depth adjustment

You may not need shelves that are 16 inches deep—even record albums require only 12½ inches. For variety, consider running each box over the table saw to trim off 3 or 4 inches. You can also use a circular saw with an edge guide. Check for nails or staples and remove them, if possible, before making cuts. Wear eye protection in any case.

To create a pyramid effect, set a row of full-size boxes on the bottom, then cut each successive row an inch or two shallower than the one below it. Emphasize the effect by painting the cubes in each row successively lighter or darker tones.

Storage details

Cubes can be modified in a number of ways to meet particular storage needs. Although manufacturers offer several variations, here are a few ideas you can build in yourself.

Shelves. Hang shelves by drilling 2 rows of ¼-inch blind holes on inside faces of cube. (Blind holes means that you should not drill the holes completely through to the outside surface.) Carefully match holes on each side to ensure that shelves will be level. Make shelves from ½-inch plywood, and support them on dowels or shelf supports plugged into holes.

Racks. Build separate racks or organizers to slip into cube to store such things as wine bottles (see the wine rack project shown on page 63).

Doors. Add doors to front of cube. A number of doors are discussed on pages 42–49.

For hinged doors, consider adding the face frame discussed on page 74, because particleboard does not adequately hold small screws, such as those used with hinges.

Drawers. Build custom drawers to hold items such as cassettes, boxes of transparencies, or spools of thread. Make simple wooden guides for the drawers, or install manufactured roller guides for effortless operation.

Edge treatments

Since the front edges are the most visible part, finish them carefully.

Wood tape veneer. Consider applying wood tape veneer to the edges. Try to get ⅝-inch-wide tape, which matches the dimension of the cube, or buy ¾-inch-wide tape and trim it after it is applied. Attach with contact cement. Overlap veneer at corners and trim through both pieces at the same time to create a clean miter. Trim overhang with a router and veneer trimming bit, or use a knife.

Half-round. Half-round applied to the front edges will soften the shape of the box and hide the relatively rough texture of the particleboard. Choose ⅝-inch-diameter strips to cover the entire edge or a smaller diameter for a more elaborate look.

Carefully miter corners, then attach strips with glue and brads. Countersink brads with a set, fill the holes, then sand. Finish as desired.

Molding. Any screen molding or beading ⅝ inch or less will also dress up the boxes. Attach it to the cubes as described above.

Scores. Cut a shadow-line groove into front edges. Set table-saw fence so that you can run each box over the blade and cut a centered kerf ¹/₁₆ to ³/₃₂ inch deep.

Inlays. Cut a kerf as described above and glue in a thin strip of molding or length of thin dowel. Finish inlays and carefully miter corners before gluing in place.

Face frames. Build face frames for some or all of the cubes. Choose a hardwood for good looks and durability. Attach face frames to cubes with glue and finishing nails.

Corner treatments

To create the appearance of a campaign chest, use brads or small round-head screws to attach metal corners to boxes. Corners are available in plated steel or brass, and can be easily spray-painted. Apply them after box is painted.

Surface treatments

When painting particleboard cubes, or particleboard in general, realize that the material is very absorbent and a sealer or primer is highly recommended. The board has more surface texture than most woods, and although it is usually sanded smooth, exposure to moisture will dramatically increase the texture. Don't let even a few raindrops hit the cubes as you unload them from your car. Sealers and primers should be applied with a brush but spraying is the best and fastest way to apply the final finish. Consider a speckled finish for cubes. A variety of these finishes are available from the Zolatone company, or as trunk paint from auto stores.

Finishing edges

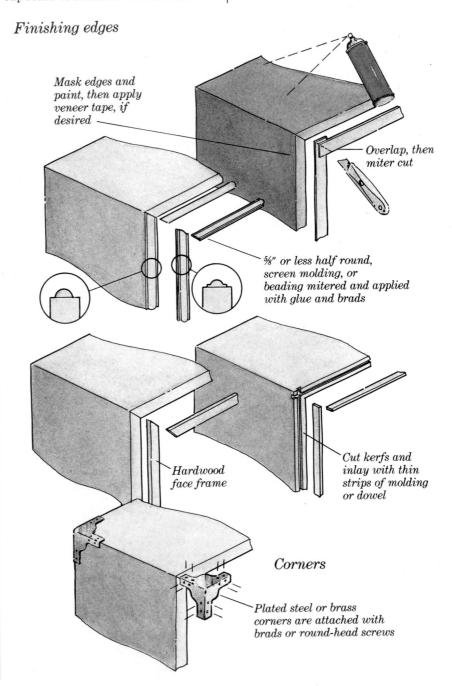

Mask edges and paint, then apply veneer tape, if desired

Overlap, then miter cut

⅝" or less half round, screen molding, or beading mitered and applied with glue and brads

Hardwood face frame

Cut kerfs and inlay with thin strips of molding or dowel

Corners

Plated steel or brass corners are attached with brads or round-head screws

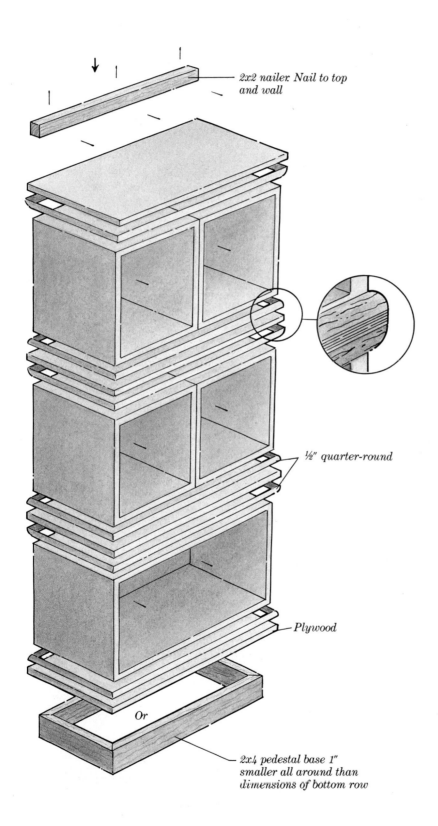

2x2 nailer. Nail to top and wall

½" quarter-round

Plywood

Or

2x4 pedestal base 1" smaller all around than dimensions of bottom row

Stabilizing a wall of cubes

Since the cubes are individual elements, a whole wall of them could actually be dangerous if you fail to take precautions to stabilize them. Here are three things you can do.

1. Sandwich sheets of board or plywood between the horizontal rows of cubes. Cut sheets 1 inch larger than the cube in all directions, and attach lengths of ½-inch quarter-round to plywood edges. The quarter-round will act as a retainer to keep the cubes in position. When well finished, these stabilizers enhance the general appearance of the cube structure.

2. Build a base. The simplest way is to lay dark-colored 2 by 4s parallel to each other and stack cubes on top. For a more finished look, build a pedestal base. A pedestal is particularly recommended when cubes are stacked on carpeted floors. Using 2 by 4s, build a base 1 inch smaller all around than the dimensions of the bottom row of cubes. Lay boards either flat or on edge, depending on how high you wish the toe kick and the unit to be.

3. When cubes are stacked more than 4 high (less if children might climb on them), attach them to the wall. (Any wall system that is not built-in should be tied to the wall, preferably into the studs.) Attach a 2 by 2 nailer across the back edge of the top row, then nail this into the wall.

OPEN UTILITY SHELVES

These shelves, although lacking in elegance, make excellent quick shelving in a garage or potting shed.

They can be made from a variety of materials, including pine, fir, or redwood, and depending on your needs, you can build them low, high, or sized to sit on top of or fasten above a workbench or counter.

If you have the pieces of wood cut at the lumberyard, making these shelves requires minimal woodworking skills. The fasteners can be metal or plastic channels formed in T, L, and X shapes designed to join 1-by boards or standard L brackets of formed steel.

If you will store heavy items or wish to build a large shelf unit, then 2-by lumber is the appropriate stock for the structural parts of the case such as the sides and top and bottom pieces. Shelf clips will not fit on 2-by stock, but L brackets will, as will flat steel brackets available in many shapes including L's, T's, and X's.

Since glue is not used in the construction of these simple shelves, they will eventually loosen as the wood dries and shrinks. Usage also lessens their stability. To keep shelves rigid, simply nail a sheet of ¼-inch plywood to the back of the unit. Prevent a tall unit from falling forward by attaching it to the wall near the top of the case.

Using 1-by stock

The following instructions are for building a basic shelf unit that measures 32 inches tall, 42 inches wide, and 11¼ inches deep. Substitute other dimensions if you want a case of a different size.
1. Select 1 by 12 boards in the wood of your choice. Many lumberyards have vertical bins of pine shelving, kiln-dried vertical-grain fir, and S4S (sanded 4 sides) KD redwood.
2. Cut (or have the lumberyard cut)

boards to the following sizes: 1 top at 42 inches; 3 verticals at 31¼ inches; and 4 shelves at 19⅞ inches.
3. Purchase connectors and brads or screws required to secure connectors in place: 4 L's; 10 T's; and 4 X's.
4. Select and cut a sheet of ¼-inch plywood to 32 inches by 42 inches. This plywood is optional. Under most circumstances clips will make shelving sturdy enough. You can add a plywood back later if necessary.
5. Before assembly, apply a finish to the shelves. Note that metal or plastic clips can be spray-painted to provide a bit of color or to prevent rust. Assemble pieces as shown and that's it—almost instant shelving!

Using 2-by stock

If built in redwood, these shelves can be used outdoors. Follow these steps

for a heavy-duty shelf unit 36 inches high and 42 inches wide.
1. From 2 by 12 stock, select and cut 1 top at 42 inches, 2 shelves at 39 inches, and 2 verticals at 34½ inches.
2. Decide on the type of connectors to use, and buy 8 L brackets or 4 flat steel L's and 8 flat T's. Steel connectors come in many sizes. If you are unsure about what size to buy, inform the salesperson of the intended function and size of the unit and ask for recommendations. Be sure to buy enough flat-head wood screws for all the holes in the connectors.
3. Choose and cut a ¼-inch plywood back to 41½ inches by 35½ inches. (This size allows for a ¼-inch setback at the edges.) A plywood back is strongly recommended if you use standard L brackets; it may be unnecessary if you use flat steel connectors.
4. Apply a finish to the pieces, then assemble unit as shown.

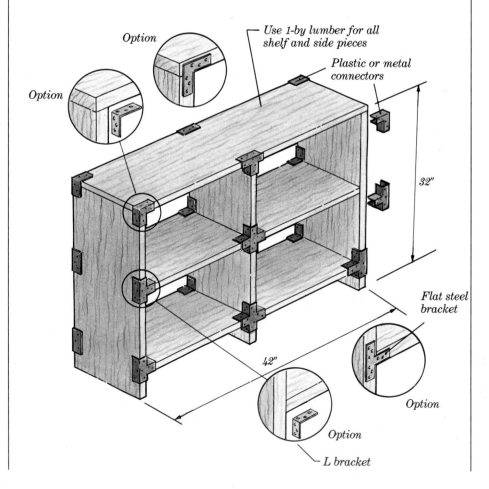

Option

Option

Option

Use 1-by lumber for all shelf and side pieces

Plastic or metal connectors

32"

42"

Flat steel bracket

Option

Option

L bracket

FIXED-SHELF UTILITY CASE

Not only does this case have a more finished appearance than the open utility shelves, but it is constructed so that it is possible to enclose the shelf space, giving you the opportunity to make this a cabinet.

The simplest way to enclose one or more of the shelves is to install sliding doors (see page 47). You should realize that since this design does not include a face frame, it is unsuitable to hang large, hinged doors.

Dimensions for the unit shown here are 36 inches tall by 36 inches wide by 11¼ inches deep, but as with all of the projects in this chapter, you can adjust the size according to your own needs. In addition to basic tools (including a carpenter's square), a router, table saw, or radial arm saw is highly recommended for cutting rabbets and dadoes.

1. From 1 by 12 board stock, cut 1 top and 2 shelves at 35¼ inches and 2 sides at 36 inches. From a 1 by 4 board, cut a kickplate at 34½ inches. From ¼-inch plywood, cut a panel for the back measuring 35¼ inches by 35⅝ inches.

2. Cut a rabbet and dadoes in each side piece, making each cut ⅜ inch deep and ¾ inch wide. Position bottom dado 3½ inches up from bottom of each board so that kickplate will later fit into place. Make dadoes for center shelf at a suitable height.

3. Cut rabbets for plywood back panel at inside back edge of each side panel. These rabbets are all ¼ inch deep (to match ¼-inch-thick plywood) and ⅜ inch wide. Cut another rabbet along bottom back edge of top piece of case.

4. Rip-cut ¼ inch from back edge of center and bottom shelves to provide clearance for plywood back.

5. Using glue and 4d finishing nails, assemble the 5 pieces of 1 by 12 in the configuration shown. Nail joints to secure them, and be sure to square the case up before the glue has set.

6. When glue has set (let it sit overnight), glue and nail in back panel and kickplate.

7. Set and fill nail holes and any cracks, sand case, and apply the finish of your choice.

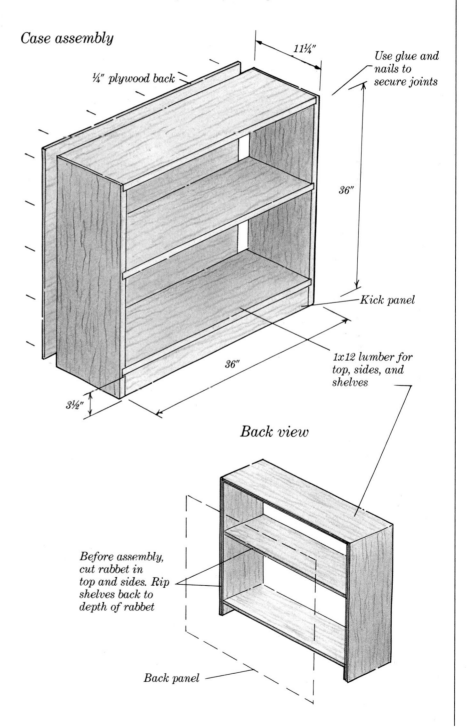

Case assembly

¼" plywood back

11¼"

Use glue and nails to secure joints

36"

Kick panel

36"

3½"

1x12 lumber for top, sides, and shelves

Back view

Before assembly, cut rabbet in top and sides. Rip shelves back to depth of rabbet

Back panel

SIMPLE PLYWOOD CABINET

T*he size of the cabi-net shown makes it suitable for use as a taboret, credenza, or even a bedside cabinet. Simple to build, it can be made of fir plywood or even particleboard. However, if you make the cabinet from quality materials, hardwood plywood for ex-ample, the result will have a handsome, profes-sionally finished look.*

Few tools are required. Rabbets, grooves, and dadoes normally used in a cabinet of this type have been replaced by nailers and cleats, thus eliminating the need for a table saw. If the lumberyard cuts the plywood for you, the only tools required for construction are a hammer, combination square, tape measure, simple mi-ter box, saw, and some clamps.

Materials list

From ¾-inch sheet material cut (or have cut): 1 top at 24¼ inches by 14⅛ inches, 2 sides at 13¼ inches by 21¾ inches, 1 bottom at 22½ inches by 13 inches, 1 shelf at 22½ inches by 12½ inches, and 2 doors at 11¹⁵⁄₁₆ inches by 21¹¹⁄₁₆ inches.

From ¼-inch plywood, cut a back panel 22½ inches by 21¾ inches.

You will also need a 72-inch-long piece of 2 by 4 for the pedestal base (get a straight board without knots), 120 inches of ¾-inch-square molding for making cleats, 20 feet of ¾-inch-wide wood tape veneer (to match the plywood selected), and hardware.

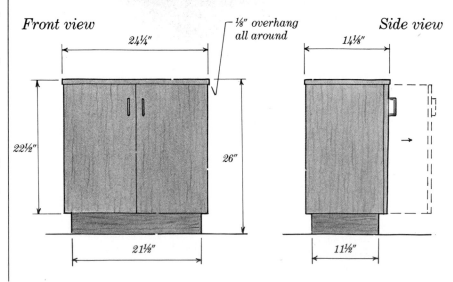

Front view

24¼"

⅛" overhang all around

22½"

26"

21½"

Side view

14⅛"

11½"

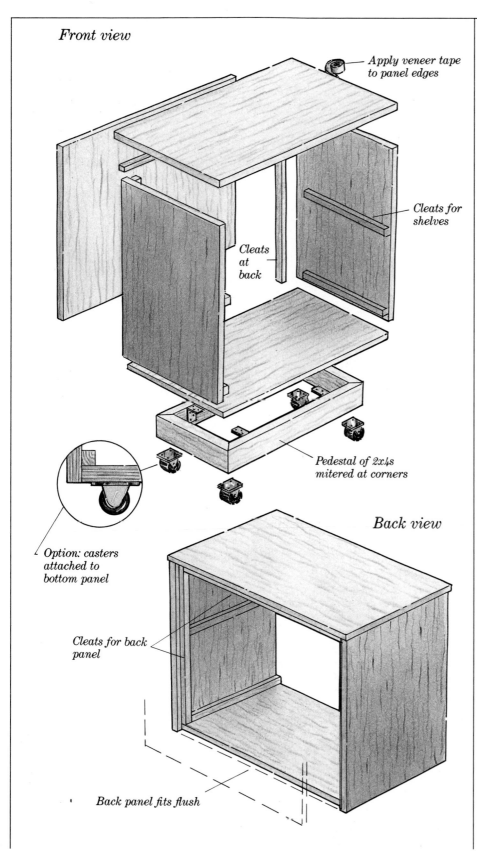

Front view

Apply veneer tape
to panel edges

Cleats for
shelves

Cleats
at
back

Pedestal of 2x4s
mitered at corners

Option: casters
attached to
bottom panel

Back view

Cleats for back
panel

Back panel fits flush

Assembling the pieces

1. Cut cleats to length as follows:
On bottom face of top panel: 2 cleats set back ⅞ inch from right and left edges.
On each side panel: 1 vertical placed ¼ inch from back edge; 1 horizontal for shelf set 10 inches down from the top edge; 1 horizontal placed ¾ inch up from bottom edge.

Cut cleats as you need them, referring to illustration for correct placement. Apply glue to cleats and, using 3d finishing nails, attach them to inside face of each piece.

2. Apply veneer edge tape to front and side edges of top panel and to all 4 sides of each door panel.

3. Check pieces for fit (but don't attach them). Sand and finish pieces.

4. Assemble by gluing and clamping panels against cleats you already attached. Unless you have 8 clamps, glue each joint and wait for glue to set before moving on to next joint. As you assemble pieces, pay close attention to the way they overlap and overhang. Set in back panel last. Secure it in place with glue and finishing nails.

5. Cut appropriate mortises for hinges, and install doors, pulls, and catches.

6. From the 2 by 4 board, cut 2 pieces at 21½ inches and 2 pieces at 11½ inches for the pedestal base. Depending on the desired height, lay 2 by 4 either flat or on edge. Miter ends of each piece. Stain or paint assembled base and attach it to bottom of cabinet with small L brackets.

FREESTANDING BOOKCASE

This design has an el-
egant simplicity, yet
the construction is
complex enough to offer
an interesting challenge
as well as the opportunity
to master a number of
woodworking techniques.

As shown here, the bookcase is 36 inches wide by 60 inches high. You may want to alter the size so that it fits your particular space. If so, consider the lines and proportions of the room in which it will stand. A bookcase that is the same height as the door, for instance, or that aligns with the tops of the window frames, will be a har-monious addition.

Shelves longer than 30 inches are likely to sag unless they are rein-forced. If you want a wider bookcase, think about adapting the design to

make the shelves stronger and more rigid. (See page 36 for a list of ways to increase the load-bearing capacity of a shelf.) Another option is to build two bookcases and stand them side by side, thereby creating the illusion of a single, larger unit.

This bookcase has a face frame to make it more rigid and to cover ex-posed edges of plywood. This is not a structural element. The case can also be constructed from either 1-by or 2-by solid lumber.

Building the case

1. Rip a sheet of ¾-inch oak plywood into 3 strips, each 11 inches wide. From these strips, cut 2 side panels, each 60 inches long; and 1 top and 1 base, each 29¼ inches long.
2. Rip plywood shelves to 10½ inches wide. Shelves are narrower than other pieces to allow for the ¼-inch back and the ¼-inch shelf edging. Cut 4 pieces, each 29¼ inches long.
3. Lay 2 side panels side by side with top and bottom edges lined up. On inside faces, measure and mark position of top piece (¾ inch from top edge) and bottom shelf (1½ inches from bottom edge). Carefully join marks across full width of both boards. These are the guidelines for cutting rabbets at the top and dadoes at the bottom, so make sure that they are square and true and that side pieces match exactly.
4. Mark positions for the 4 shelves in the same way. In this bookcase, shelves are placed 15, 27, 39, and 50 inches from the bottom, but these positions can be changed to suit.
5. Cut ¾-inch-wide by ⅜-inch-deep dadoes to accommodate shelves and a ⅜-inch rabbet in each side panel to accept top.
6. Cut ¼-inch-wide by ⅜-inch-deep rabbets along back edges of top, sides, and bottom. These will accommodate back panel.

Edging the shelves

1. From 1 by 2 solid oak, rip 4 strips, each ¼ inch thick by ¾ inch wide, for shelf edging. Cut strips the same length as shelves.
2. Apply a light coat of glue to front edge of each shelf, then nail on edging, placing a finishing nail at each end and one in the middle. Set nail heads and fill holes.
3. When glue is dry, scrape off excess and sand carefully so that edging is flush with plywood surface.

Assembling the case

1. On one side piece, apply a small amount of glue to top rabbet. Set top piece in rabbet, making sure that rabbet in back panel lines up with the one in side piece. Cross-nail top to side, using 4 nails driven alternately from sides and from top. Position outermost nails about ½ to ¾ inch from each edge.
2. Apply a little glue to dado for bottom piece. Set bottom piece into place, making sure that ¼-inch rabbet is at the back, face up. Nail from outside to secure bottom.
3. Apply a little glue to dadoes for shelves. Seat each shelf well into groove so that edge facing of shelf is flush with front edge of side piece.
4. Nail shelves into place from the outside, using 2 finishing nails on both ends of each shelf.
5. Apply glue to rabbet and dadoes of second side piece. Carefully fit top, bottom, and shelves into place. Check case for square and nail pieces in place.
6. From a sheet of ¼-inch-thick plywood, cut back panel to 29¼ inches by 58¼ inches. Sand side of back panel that will be exposed to view.
7. From back of bookcase, nail panel into place, squaring it as you go.
8. Clamp case and allow glue to dry.

Case assembly

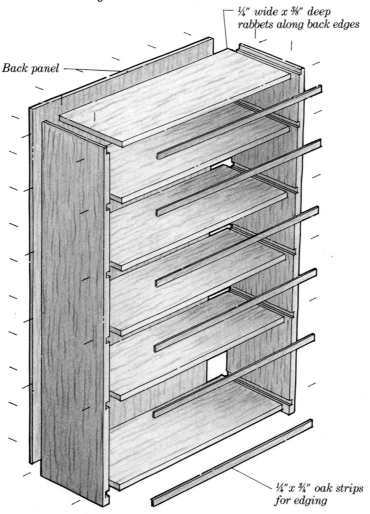

Back panel

¼" wide x ⅜" deep rabbets along back edges

¼" x ¾" oak strips for edging

Making the face frame

1. From 1 by 2 oak, cut 2 stiles (vertical pieces) to 60 inches long and 2 rails (horizontal pieces) to length. (Rails should fit exactly inside stiles when stiles are flush with outside edges of case—approximately 27 inches. Measure to be sure.)
2. On a flat surface, align rails squarely inside stiles. Mark 2 lines across each joint with a pencil and square. These are the guidelines for placing dowels.
3. Using an adjustable doweling jig, drill holes to accept ¼-inch dowels, making them slightly more than 1 inch deep.
4. Apply glue along end grain and in dowel holes in rails. Tap in dowels.
5. Put glue in dowel holes in stiles. Tap assembly together.
6. Check face frame for square, clamp it, and let glue dry.
7. Apply adhesive to exposed plywood edges on front of bookcase. Fit face frame to case so that all outside edges are flush and bottom rail aligns with top of lowest shelf. Nail face frame into place and clamp it.
8. Set nails and fill holes. Let case dry. When glue is completely dry, scrape off excess and sand entire case. Finish it as desired.

Pedestal base

A pedestal base will give the bookcase a less massive appearance by creating a shadow and a sense of space beneath it. You can make a base out of the extra strip of plywood from which you cut the bookcase components.

Assembling the base

1. Cut a 5-inch-wide by 96-inch-long plywood strip in half. (Two 48-inch lengths are easier to handle when you are cutting in a miter box.)
2. Place one 48-inch length in miter box and cut 1 piece 10¾ inches long and 1 piece 28⅜ inches long. Cut 45-degree miters at both ends. (Given length refers to longest side.) Cut other 48-inch-long piece in the same way.
3. Apply glue to end grain of miters on 1 short piece and 1 long piece. Fit them together and cross-nail with finishing nails. Set nail heads. Fasten the other 2 pieces together in the same way, then fasten the 2 L-shaped pieces to each other. Check for square, clamp, and allow to dry.

Clean off excess glue, fill nail holes, sand, and finish.
4. Put pedestal in place. Set bookcase on it so that bottom shelf sits on pedestal and face frame and sides overlap pedestal.

Bookcase should be very stable when you set it on the base. However, if you desire, you can attach the 2 pieces together with L brackets.

Face frame

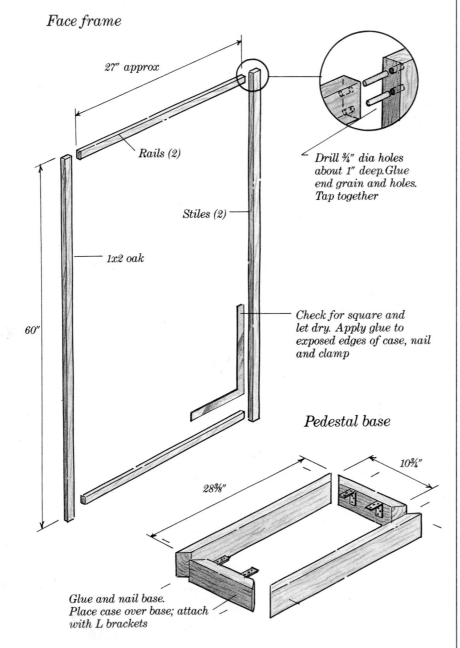

27″ approx

Rails (2)

Stiles (2)

1x2 oak

60″

Drill ¾″ dia holes about 1″ deep. Glue end grain and holes. Tap together

Check for square and let dry. Apply glue to exposed edges of case, nail and clamp

Pedestal base

10¾″

28⅜″

Glue and nail base. Place case over base; attach with L brackets

TALL PINE BOOKCASE

T raditional in appearance, and made with modest materials, this pine bookcase will be perfectly at home in a casual setting. It is constructed from standard-sized rack pine boards and stock molding.

Materials needed

The sides and shelves of this case are made from 1 by 12 pine shelving. Nearly all lumberyards have bins of this material. When selecting boards, bear in mind that, although a few knots will add charm to your project, you should try to find wood that is free from large, loose, or numerous knots. You will need two 72-inch side pieces and enough board to cut 24-inch-long pieces for the top, bottom, and each shelf.

Building the basic case

1. Cut ¾-inch-wide by ⅜-inch-deep dadoes and rabbets on side pieces to accept top and bottom panels.

Along back inside edges of both side pieces and the top piece, cut ¼-inch-wide by ⅜-inch-deep rabbets to accept back panel.

2. Measure and drill 2 rows of holes into each side piece for the shelf supports. Space holes 2 inches apart in vertical rows 1½ inches from front and back edges. Use a drill guide with a stop to prevent drilling completely through sides.

3. Rip-cut ¼ inch from the piece that forms the bottom shelf so that back panel will fit.

4. Assemble top, bottom, and sides using glue and 4d finishing nails. Make sure bottom shelf is seated in dado, check for square, and let dry.

5. Measure the size for the back panel. It should fit into rabbets cut at back of main assembly and overlap back of bottom shelf. Cut a piece of ¼-inch plywood to fit, and fasten it with glue and 2d finishing nails.

Applying the trim

Pine lath in several widths is generally available from the lumberyard. Buy the sanded 4-side (S4S) variety, not rough lath used in plastering. Where pieces of wide lath are edge-glued together at top and bottom of face frame, back up the joint on the inside with another piece of lath.

1. Edge-glue enough lath together to make 4-inch by 24¾-inch pieces for both top and bottom of face frame. If you desire a decorative cutout in the top piece, as shown in the illustration, make it now. Glue and nail top piece to main assembly, attaching it 1 inch down from the top.

If large doors are part of your design, make the face frame from 1-by stock rather than lath.

2. Lay 1-inch-wide side pieces of lath in place, butted against upper piece already attached to case. Mark position of top surface of bottom shelf and

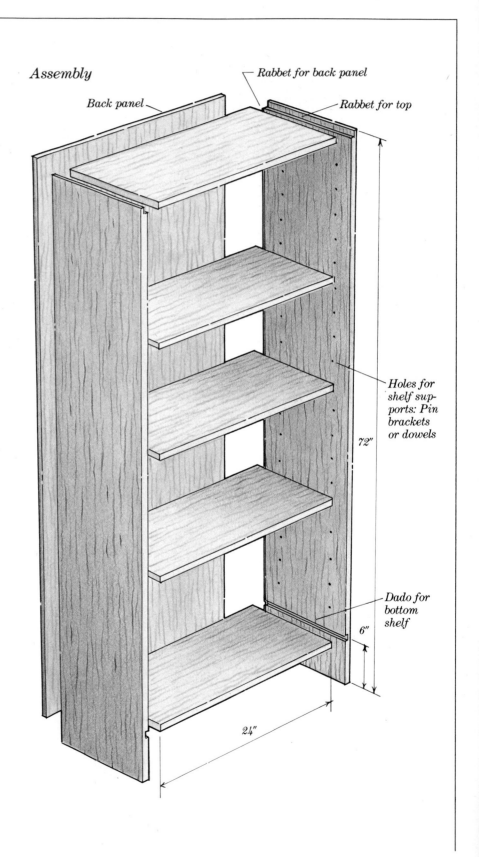

Assembly

Back panel

Rabbet for back panel

Rabbet for top

Holes for shelf supports: Pin brackets or dowels

72"

Dado for bottom shelf

6"

24"

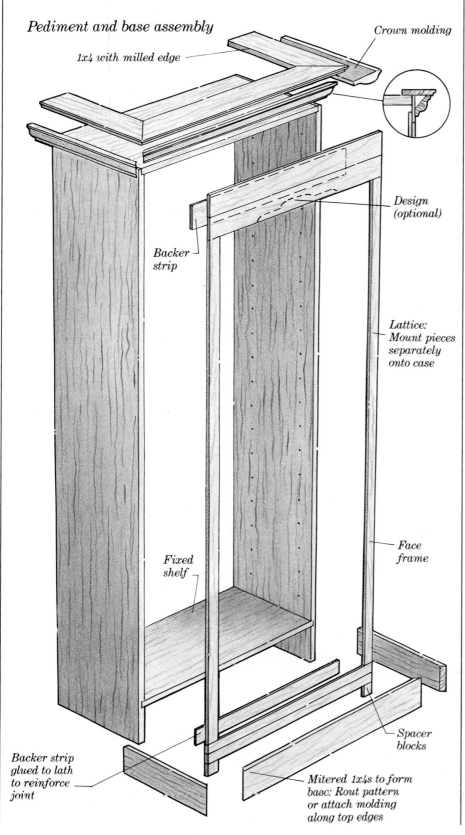

Pediment and base assembly

1x4 with milled edge

Crown molding

Design
(optional)

Backer
strip

Lattice:
Mount pieces
separately
onto case

Fixed
shelf

Face
frame

Spacer
blocks

Backer strip
glued to lath
to reinforce
joint

Mitered 1x4s to form
base: Rout pattern
or attach molding
along top edges

cut side pieces to fit. Glue and nail lath to sides, flush with outside edges. 3. Glue and nail remaining part of face frame into position against bottom edges of side pieces. Make top edge flush with top of bottom panel.

Pediment and base molding

When creating the pediment for this cabinet, you may find it easier to join the crown molding to the 1 by 4, as shown, let glue set, and cut the 3 sections needed in a miter box or with a radial arm saw. The alternative is to cut and fit pieces separately, but this increases the chance for error. If you use the latter method, cut and attach the 1 by 4s first.
1. Glue together pieces needed for pediment. Cut front piece of crown molding assembly first, making miters at both ends. Make sure that shorter edge equals outside case dimension. Cut miters at front ends of side pieces, hold them against case, and mark correct length. Make straight cuts at this mark, and attach side pieces of pediment to case.
2. Measure and cut base molding in the same manner as crown molding, also starting with piece at front. Attach pieces to case with glue and 4d finishing nails.

Finishing details

1. Measure and cut as many shelf boards as needed (4 or 5 should be sufficient). Length of each board depends on type of shelf supports to be used. Rip $5/16$ inch off each shelf to allow for thickness of back panel. If you are not installing shelves, plan interior divisions and inserts now, and install them.
2. Countersink all nails with a nail set, then fill holes and any gaps. When the filler is dry, sand whole project, and apply finish of your choice.

STANDARD BASE CABINET

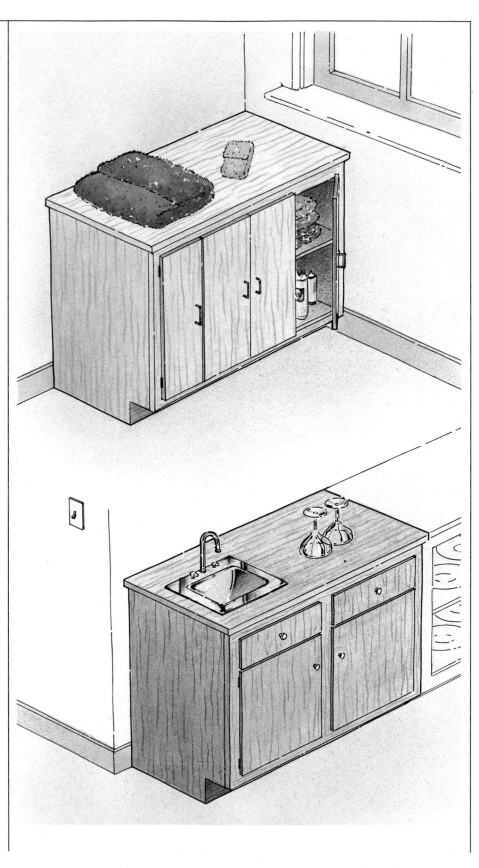

*S*caled-up version of this cabinet design is often used for built-ins such as kitchen cabinets. This case can also be freestanding.

The basic dimensions of the cabinet shown are 36 inches wide by 30 inches high by 18 inches deep. The cabinet can be built in the material of your choice and all dimensions can be changed to suit.

Building sides and base

1. From ¾-inch stock, cut 2 panels 17¼ inches by 29¼ inches. Cut a 3½-inch-square notch at lower front corner of each panel, creating a mirrored pair.
2. On inner side of each panel, rout a ¾-inch-wide by ¼-inch-deep groove from front to back. Bottom edge of groove should be even with top of the 3½-inch cutout. These grooves will support the bottom panel. Cut a ⅜-inch-wide by ¼-inch-deep rabbet on the inside back edge of each side piece. These rabbets will accept the ¼-inch plywood back panel. Rout additional grooves if you plan to install any fixed shelves; drill holes for adjustable shelf supports.
3. From ¾-inch sheet material, cut a base panel 35 inches by 17 inches. From 1 by 2 stock, cut a 34½-inch-long nailer.
4. Carefully assemble pieces as shown, using glue and 4d finishing nails. Check square before glue sets.

Making the face frame

Normally constructed of 1 by 2 wood, the face frame is one of the most visible parts of the cabinet and also provides support for hanging doors.

When planning the face frame, remember that the edging that you will attach to the top panel overlaps the

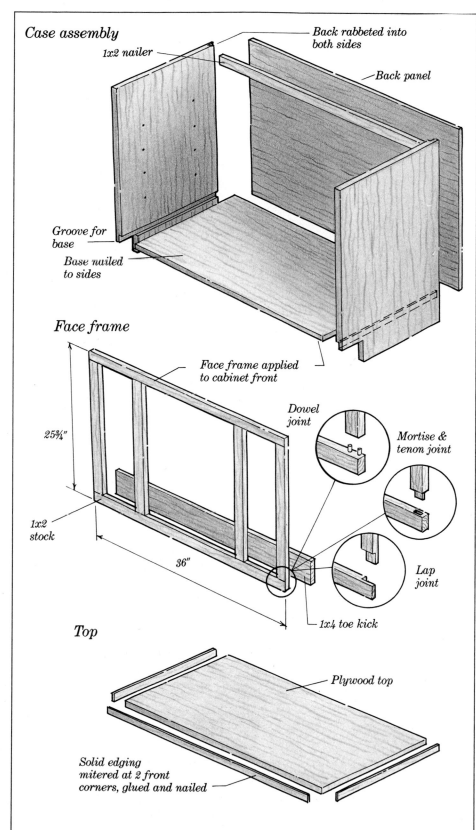

Case assembly

1x2 nailer

Back rabbeted into both sides

Back panel

Groove for base

Base nailed to sides

Face frame

Face frame applied to cabinet front

Dowel joint

Mortise & tenon joint

25¾"

1x2 stock

36"

Lap joint

1x4 toe kick

Top

Plywood top

Solid edging mitered at 2 front corners, glued and nailed

---

upper portion of the face frame. If the overlap will be particularly deep, adjust dimension of top rail of face frame accordingly.

1. Lay out parts of face frame, carefully making sure that outside dimensions are 36 inches wide by 25¾ inches high. Correct measurements are critical as the frame determines the door and drawer openings.

Any of several types of joints may be used to join the corners; a few are illustrated.

2. Tip previously assembled portion of case onto its back. Before setting face frame in place, cut and fit a piece of 1 by 4 across bottom for the toe kick. Secure it in place with glue and 4d finishing nails.

3. Attach face frame to front of case using glue and 4d finishing nails.

Attaching the top

If you plan to use this cabinet in the kitchen, consider finishing off the top with plastic laminate or ceramic tile. A natural wood top may make the cabinet conform to the style of the living areas of your home.

1. Measure outside dimensions of cabinet and add at least ¹/₁₆ inch, more if you want a larger overhang. From ¾-inch plywood, cut top panel to these dimensions.

2. Carefully cut three 1 by 2 edging strips. Since these strips are attached to side and front edges of top, where they are visible, take care to miter corners for a precise fit.

Attach strips flush with top surface of top panel unless you plan to tile the surface. If this is the case, overlap top surface by the depth of the tile to create an edging. Secure strips to top edge with glue and finishing nails.

Finishing touches

You are now ready to set all nails, fill holes and gaps, and sand the cabinet. However, before applying the finish, add the doors, drawers, shelves, trays, and dividers selected from the "Adding Features" chapter.

INTERLOCKING SHELVES

If you are always looking for bookends to
keep long rows of
books divided into sec-
tions, consider this case.
These storage boxes utilize
the time-tested concept of
interlocking boards as the
basis for a system of storage boxes that can be
scaled to suit almost any
storage need.

The project shown is built from
plywood and is based on a 12-inch
cubic module. If you plan to store
record albums or a collection of dolls,
for instance, design your own system
of interlocking shelves based on a
suitable module.

The number of boxes, as well as
the size, is variable. The unit shown
has 24 boxes, but using the same
principle, you can make a case with
as few as 4 or as many as needed for
a whole wall of storage. To stabilize
the unit, you may have to build a
base to put under it. To keep tall units
from tipping forward, attach top to
wall using a cleat screwed into wall
studs, which is then nailed or
screwed to the top of the case.

Shelf dimensions

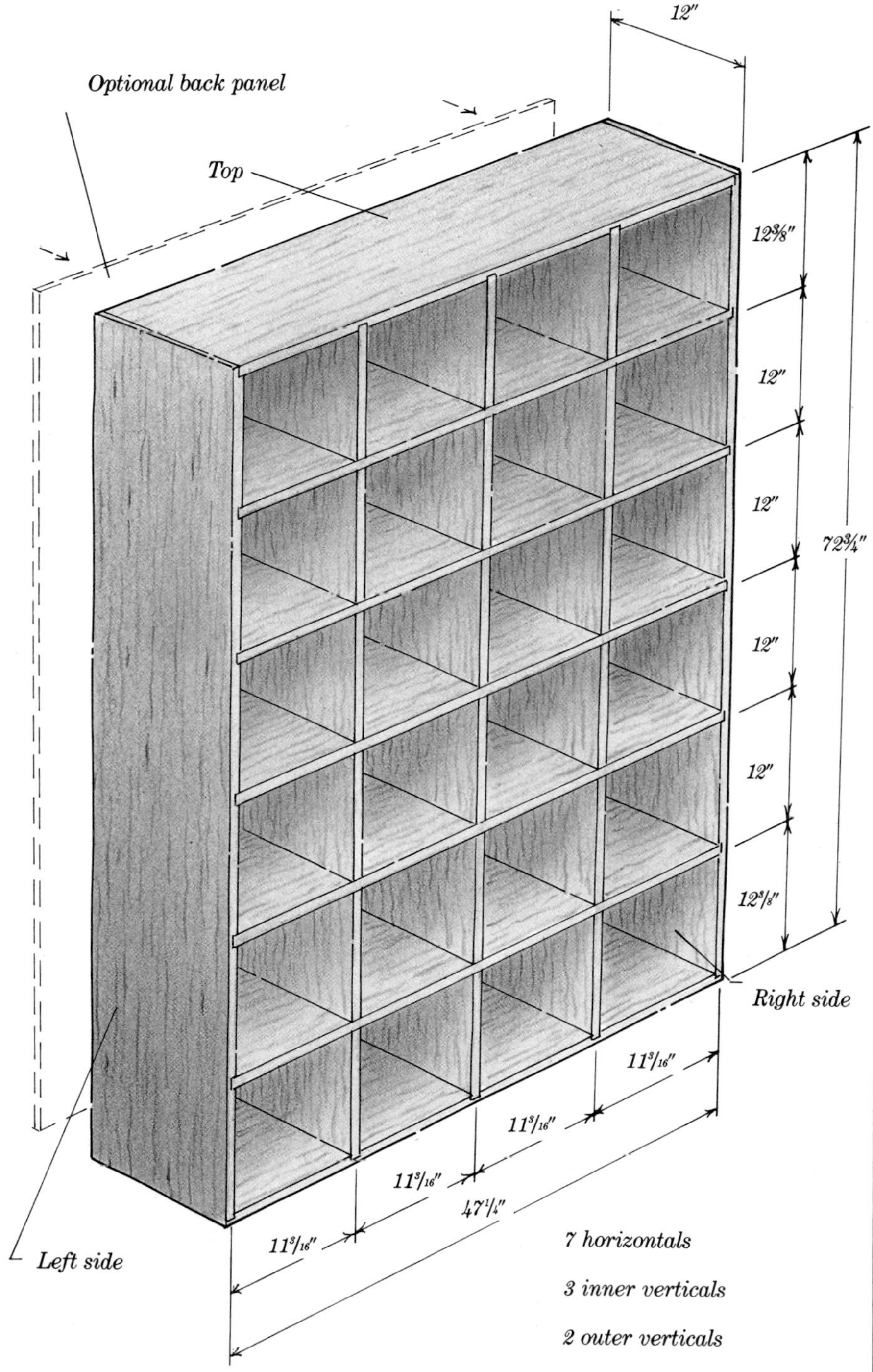

Optional back panel

Top

12"

12⅜"

12"

12"

72¾"

12"

12"

12⅜"

Right side

11³/₁₆"

11³/₁₆"

11³/₁₆"

11³/₁₆"

47¼"

Left side

7 horizontals

3 inner verticals

2 outer verticals

Materials needed

The unit shown is constructed from 12-inch strips of solid-core plywood. Plywood was chosen for its strength as much as for its looks. The whole unit could also be slightly scaled down in order to use 1 by 12 pine shelving. However, because notches are cut halfway through each board in several places, the weaker pine shelving can break once shelves are put into service. To get around this problem, add a plywood back, driving nails into back edges of shelves.

Building techniques

Whether you include a plywood back or not, follow this procedure.
1. Cut 4 outer pieces (top, bottom, and 2 sides) ¼ inch deeper than shelf boards and vertical dividers.
2. Cut a ¾-inch rabbet in each outer board. On the inner back edge of each outer board, cut a rabbet ¼ inch deep and ⅜ inch wide.
3. If more than 1 sheet of plywood is needed for back panel, cut plywood so that joints fall where they will be obscured by a vertical divider.

Building a 24-cube unit

1. From each of 3 sheets of ¾-inch hardwood plywood stock, cut 3 strips 12 inches wide by 96 inches long (9 strips in total).
2. From 12-inch-wide strips, cut 2 outer vertical panels 72¾ inches long, 3 inner vertical dividers 72 inches long, and 7 horizontal panels 47¼ inches long.
3. Select 4 of these strips for top, bottom, and sides of case, and mark them very accurately for rabbets and dadoes. Dimensions shown on illustration are from ends of individual boards to center points of dadoes. This means that rabbets will be inset from ends of boards, and dadoes will be centered on their marks.
4. Using a ¾-inch wide dado blade or router bit, cut ⅜-inch-deep rabbets and dadoes.

5. Cut notches in remaining horizontal pieces. Lay out notches to correspond exactly to locations of dadoes you previously cut into top and bottom pieces. Make notches ¾ inch wide and just over 6 inches deep. They should extend from back of board to just beyond the midpoint.

6. Cut notches in remaining vertical boards. Position these shorter boards against the outer (longer) boards to mark position of cuts. Note that half of the rabbet on each end of each outer board should extend beyond ends of shorter inner boards. This ensures that notches are in the right places. Cut these notches ¾ inch wide, from the front of each board to just beyond the midpoint.

7. Check cut pieces by aligning them with their adjacent pieces. Notches and dadoes should line up. If they fail to line up, you will have a difficult time fitting all the pieces together, although a small amount of error can be accommodated.

8. Using a rubber mallet, assemble pieces starting with the grid of inner boards. Add top and bottom pieces to inner grid, securing them in place with glue and finishing nails. Check assembly for square, do not disturb, and allow glue to dry.

9. Fit vertical side panels, securing them with glue and finishing nails. Check again for square, and allow assembly to dry. Apply the finish of your choice.

Grid can be used as is for storage. If you want to make it more of a display piece and dress it up a bit, you can add a base or pediment, as shown in the illustration.

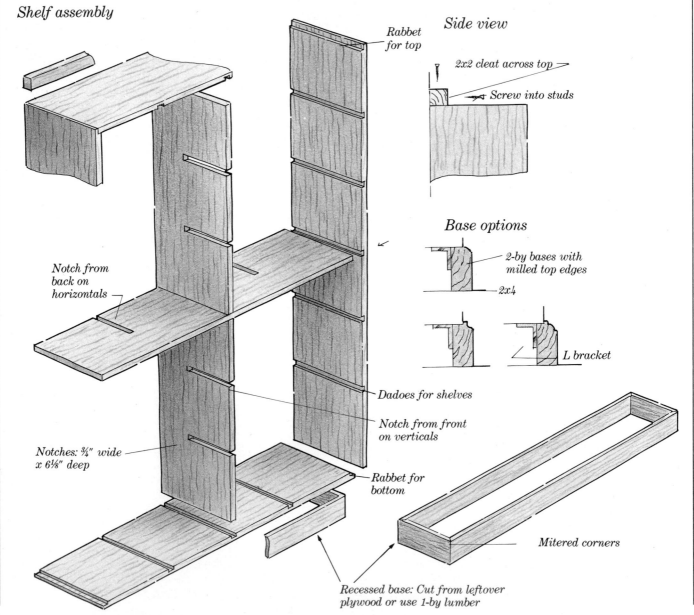

Shelf assembly

Rabbet for top

Notch from back on horizontals

Notches: ¾" wide x 6⅛" deep

Dadoes for shelves

Notch from front on verticals

Rabbet for bottom

Recessed base: Cut from leftover plywood or use 1-by lumber

Side view

2x2 cleat across top

Screw into studs

Base options

2-by bases with milled top edges

2x4

L bracket

Mitered corners

CORNER CABINET

*A*s an open case, this unit is suitable for storing books and mementos, but with doors added (see pages 42–49), it can become home for any number of items ranging from china to clothing.

Traditionally a corner cabinet or cupboard is completely triangular. This version allows for slightly longer shelves without cutting off too much of the room. It also prevents the cabinet from appearing too massive.

These shelves are greater in distance from front to back than is standard board lumber. Therefore, unless you are able to edge-glue boards together to make sheets of solid wood, build this project with plywood shelves, including top and bottom pieces. Make face frame and rear spine out of solid wood. Shelves are 19⅜ inches at the deepest point.

Forming side panels

From ¾-inch solid-core plywood or solid 1-by pine or hardwood, cut two 5½-inch-wide strips for side pieces.
1. Determine height of cabinet (72 inches is a comfortable height) and cut two 5½-inch strips to that length.
2. Rip a 45-degree rabbet along back edge of each side piece. If you are using a circular saw, this may require two passes.
3. Crosscut a rabbet at inner top of each side piece. Make rabbet ⅜ inch deep and ¾ inch wide.
4. Lay out desired pattern of shelves on inner faces of side pieces, and cut a ⅜-inch-deep by ¾-inch-wide dado for each shelf. Be sure that dadoes line up with each other when the 2 side pieces lie side by side and face up. If they don't, you will have slanted shelves!

Note that if you plan to use a 1 by 6 for bottom rail of face frame, you should cut lowest dado in side pieces so that top of dado is 5½ inches from bottom of side pieces.

Making a spine

1. Cut a 2 by 4 to the same length as side pieces you already formed.
2. Bevel-rip 2 by 4 into a trapezoidal shape by making 2 rip cuts at 45 degrees, 1 along each side of board.
3. Cut rabbet and dadoes across wide face of board to match pattern of cuts on side pieces. Use a side piece as a gauge to mark cuts on spine. Make these cuts ⅜ inch deep and ¾ inch wide.

Making shelves

Top of case is actually a shelf. It is held by rabbets cut in side pieces and spine. Shelves sit in dadoes cut into sides and spine.

From ¾-inch plywood, cut shelves and top to dimensions shown in illustration. For better appearance, attach a strip of ¼-inch by ¾-inch hardwood trim to front edge of each shelf board before making final dimensional cuts.

Assembling the case

1. Assemble main framework of case, face down. Fit 1 side piece to edges of top and shelves. Apply glue into each dado, and fit side and shelves together, making sure that shelves and side piece are flush at the front. Secure joint with finishing nails.
2. Before glue sets on first side piece, apply glue to dadoes in second side piece and fit opposite ends of shelves. Secure with finishing nails.
3. Without delay, apply glue to cuts in spine and lay spine into position at back of shelves. If cuts were accurate, everything will fit, but minor adjustments can be made before glue is set. When satisfied, nail spine to shelves. With case still face down, square it up, make sure it is not twisted, then do not disturb it until glue has set.

Attaching backing

1. Add back panels with case still face down. Measure and cut panels from ¼-inch plywood. Each panel should extend from notch at back of side panel to back edge of spine. Make top and bottom of each panel flush with top and bottom of case.
2. Apply glue to notch in side pieces and along spine. Place each back panel in position, and nail it to sides, shelves, and spine with ⅝-inch brads.

Adding face frame

1. Turn case over and measure front. Cut pieces required for face frame from 1 by 2 solid stock. Illustration shows a face frame around perimeter of case, but you could add a center stile, as well as 1 or more intermediary rails. This would allow you to attach several smaller door panels, rather than 1 or 2 large doors.
2. Join corners of face frame together. Attach frame to front of case.
3. Set nail heads, and fill holes and gaps with filler. Sand, and apply the finish of your choice.

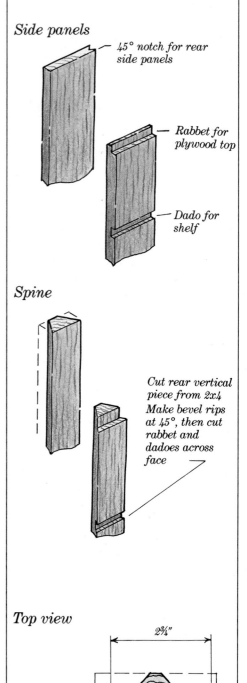

Side panels

45° notch for rear side panels

Rabbet for plywood top

Dado for shelf

Spine

Cut rear vertical piece from 2x4 Make bevel rips at 45°, then cut rabbet and dadoes across face

Top view

2¾"

45°

⅜"

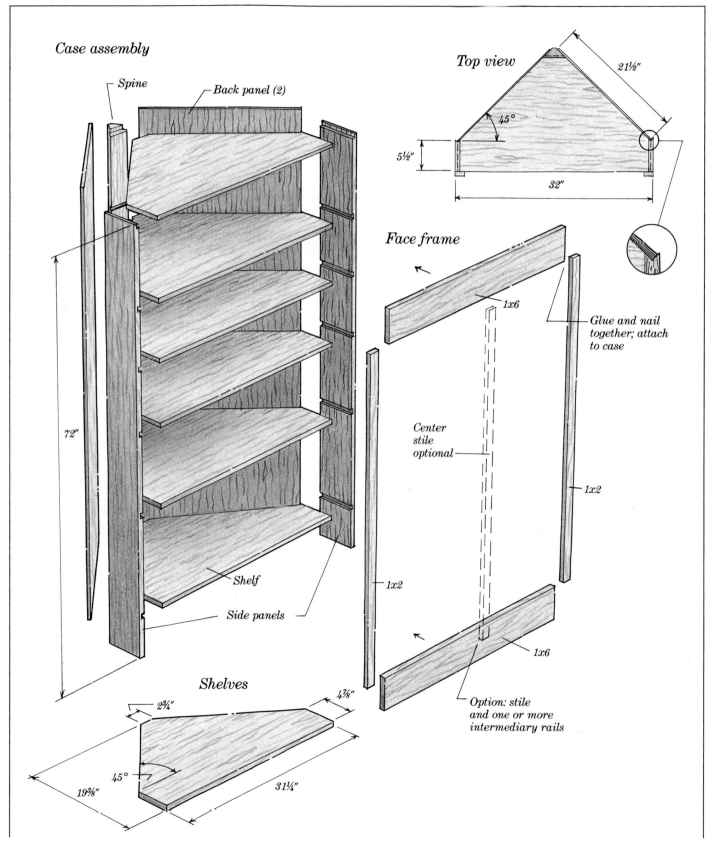

Case assembly

Spine

Back panel (2)

72"

Shelf

Side panels

Shelves

2¾"

45°

19⅜"

31¼"

4⅞"

Top view

21½"

45°

5½"

32"

Face frame

1x6

Glue and nail together; attach to case

Center stile optional

1x2

1x2

1x6

Option: stile and one or more intermediary rails

U.S. Measure and Metric Measure Conversion Chart

		Formulas for Exact Measures			Rounded Measures for Quick Reference		
	Symbol	When you know:	Multiply by	To find:			
Mass (Weight)	oz	ounces	28.35	grams	1 oz		= 30 g
	lb	pounds	0.45	kilograms	4 oz		= 115 g
	g	grams	0.035	ounces	8 oz		= 225 g
	kg	kilograms	2.2	pounds	16 oz	= 1 lb	= 450 g
					32 oz	= 2 lb	= 900 g
					36 oz	= 2 1/4 lb	= 1000g (a kg)
Volume	tsp	teaspoons	5.0	milliliters	1/4 tsp	= 1/24 oz	= 1 ml
	tbsp	tablespoons	15.0	milliliters	1/2 tsp	= 1/12 oz	= 2 ml
	fl oz	fluid ounces	29.57	milliliters	1 tsp	= 1/6 oz	= 5 ml
	c	cups	0.24	liters	1 tbsp	= 1/2 oz	= 15 ml
	pt	pints	0.47	liters	1 c	= 8 oz	= 250 ml
	qt	quarts	0.95	liters	2 c (1 pt)	= 16 oz	= 500 ml
	gal	gallons	3.785	liters	4 c (1 qt)	= 32 oz	= 1 l
	ml	milliters	0.034	fluid ounces	4 qt (1 gal)	= 128 oz	= 3 3/4 l
Length	in.	inches	2.54	centimeters	3/8 in.	= 1 cm	
	ft	feet	30.48	centimeters	1 in.	= 2.5 cm	
	yd	yards	0.9144	meters	2 in.	= 5 cm	
	mi	miles	1.609	kilometers	2-1/2 in.	= 6.5 cm	
	km	kilometers	0.621	miles	12 in. (1 ft)	= 30 cm	
	m	meters	1.094	yards	1 yd	= 90 cm	
	cm	centimeters	0.39	inches	100 ft	= 30 m	
					1 mi	= 1.6 km	
Temperature	°F	Fahrenheit	5/9 (after subtracting 32)	Celsius	32°F	= 0°C	
					68°F	= 20°C	
	°C	Celsius	9/5 (then add 32)	Fahrenheit	212°F	= 100°C	
Area	in.²	square inches	6.452	square centimeters	1 in.²	= 6.5 cm²	
	ft²	square feet	929.0	square centimeters	1 ft²	= 930 cm²	
	yd²	square yards	8361.0	square centimeters	1 yd²	= 8360 cm²	
	a	acres	0.4047	hectares	1 a	= 4050 m²	

INDEX